P9-DGJ-101

TIMELINES
OF
HISTORY
VOLUME 10

THE MODERN WORLD

1900–2000

GROLIER

an imprint of

◼SCHOLASTIC

www.scholastic.com/librarypublishing

Published by Grolier,
an imprint of Scholastic Library Publishing,
Sherman Turnpike
Danbury, Connecticut 06816

© 2005 The Brown Reference Group plc

Set ISBN 0-7172-6002-X
Volume 10 ISBN 0-7172-6012-7

Library of Congress Cataloging-in-Publication Data

Timelines of history.
        p. cm.
    Includes index.
    Contents: v. 1. The early empires, prehistory—500 B.C. —
v. 2. The classical age, 500 B.C.—500 A.D. — v. 3. Raiders and
conquerors, 500—1000 — v. 4. The feudal era, 1000—1250 —
v. 5. The end of the Middle Ages, 1250—1500 — v. 6. A wider
world, 1500—1600 — v. 7. Royalty and revolt, 1600—1700 —
v. 8. The Age of Reason, 1700—1800 — v. 9. Industry and
empire, 1800—1900 — v. 10. The modern world, 1900—2000.
    ISBN 0-7172-6002-X (set : alk. paper) — ISBN 0-7172-
6003-8 (v. 1 : alk. paper) — ISBN 0-7172-6004-6 (v. 2 : alk.
paper) — ISBN 0-7172-6005-4 (v. 3 : alk. paper) — ISBN 0-
7172-6006-2 (v. 4 : alk. paper) — ISBN 0-7172-6007-0 (v. 5 :
alk. paper) — ISBN 0-7172-6008-9 (v. 6 : alk. paper) — ISBN
0-7172-6009-7 (v. 7 : alk. paper) — ISBN 0-7172-6010-0 (v. 8
: alk.paper) — ISBN 0-7172-6011-9 (v. 9 : alk. paper) —
ISBN 0-7172-6012-7 (v. 10 : alk. paper)
    1. Chronology, Historical

For information address the publisher:
Grolier, Sherman Turnpike,
Danbury, Connecticut 06816

Printed and bound in Thailand

FOR THE BROWN REFERENCE GROUP PLC

Consultant: Professor Jeremy Black, University of Exeter

Project Editor: Tony Allan
Designers: Frankie Wood
Picture Researcher: Sharon Southren
Cartographic Editor: Tim Williams
Design Manager: Lynne Ross
Production: Alastair Gourlay, Maggie Copeland
Senior Managing Editor: Tim Cooke
Editorial Director: Lindsey Lowe
Writers: Susan Kennedy, Michael Kerrigan, Peter Lewis

PICTURE CREDITS
(t = top, b = bottom, c = center, l = left, r = right)

Cover
Corbis: Christie's Images b.

Corbis: Bettmann 15t, 18r, 19b, 24t, 25t, 32, 33b, 47b, Bohemian
Nomad Picturemakers 10, Hulton-Deutch Collection 26t, 33c,
Reuters 46bl, Peter Turnley 44b; **EasyInternetcafe Ltd:** 43; **Getty
Images:** 8t, 9b, 11, 13b, 14t, 15b, 16cr, 17b, 20t, 21b, 28r, 30r, 35,
38t, Time Life Pictures 6t, 33t, 38b, 40; **Robert Hunt Picture
Library:** 23b; **IBM:** 42tl; **Kobal Collection:** 16t; **Mary Evans
Picture Library:** 8cr; **NASA:** 45t, Marshall Space Flight Center:
36t, 37; **National Archives and Records Administration:** 23, 34,
Franklin D . Roosevelt Library 17t; **PhotoDisc:** Jeremy
Woodhouse 21t; **Photos.com:** 29t; **Photos12.com:** Collection
Cinema 18l, 19t, KEYSTONE-Pressedienst 7, Oasis 25b;
Popperfoto.co.uk: 12; **Rex Features Ltd:** 22b, Sipa Press 39, 41c,
46br, 47t, Jacques Witt 44t; **Science Photo Library:** A.Barrington
Brown 28l; **TopFoto.co.uk:** 22c, 24c, 29b, 30l, 31, 42tr, AP 27,
NASA/The Image Works 41t, Novosti 36b; **U.S. Department of
Defense:** 45b.

The Brown Reference Group has made every effort to trace
copyright holders of the pictures used in this book. Anyone
having claims to ownership not identified above is invited to
contact The Brown Reference Group.

CONTENTS

HOW TO USE THIS BOOK

INTRODUCTION

The shaping spirit of the 20th century was technological innovation. Like Aladdin's genie, technology's powers seemed almost limitless, affecting virtually every aspect of life. Transport underwent a world-shrinking revolution; whereas in 1820 people could travel no faster than a horse could gallop, by 1980 they could fly around the globe within a day. Information moved even faster, beamed around the world in seconds by transmitter and satellite. Humans had also learned to journey through space; by 1969 men had stood on the surface of the moon.

Yet the century's material advances were not an unmixed blessing. Much of the impetus driving scientific progress originated in military research: The same momentum that carried people into space also created the nuclear bomb. Technical progress in alliance with competitive nationalism brought two world wars that between them left at least 60 million people dead. Improvements in food production and medical care increased quality of life but also sparked an unsustainable population boom. Between 1900 and 2000 the number of people on the planet grew from 1.6 to six billion.

Although the colonial era came to an end, restoring self-rule to Africa and Asia, the gulf in living standards between rich and poor nations widened. For much of the century the rival ideologies of capitalism and communism competed for the loyalty of developed and undeveloped nations alike—a struggle that largely ended with the collapse of the communist Soviet Union near the century's end. By then a new questions was slowly taking shape: Had humankind the wisdom to manage a planet whose processes it could increasingly understand but not always control?

ABBREVIATIONS

mi	miles
cm	centimeters
m	meters
km	kilometers
sq. km	square kilometers
mya	million years ago
c.	about (from the Latin word circa)

A NOTE ON DATES
This set follows standard Western practice in dating events from the start of the Christian era, presumed to have begun in the year 0. Those that happened before the year 0 are listed as B.C. (before the Christian era), and those that happened after as A.D. (from the Latin Anno Domini, meaning "in the year of the Lord"). Wherever possible, exact dates are given; where there is uncertainty, the date is prefixed by the abbreviation c. (short for Latin circa, meaning "about") to show that it is approximate.

ABOUT THIS SET

This book is one of a set of ten providing timelines for world history from the beginning of recorded history up to 2000 A.D. Each volume arranges events that happened around the world within a particular period and is made up of three different types of facing two-page spreads: timelines, features, and glossary pages ("Facts at a Glance," at the back of the book). The three should be used in combination to find the information that you need. Timelines list events that occurred between the dates shown on the pages and cover periods ranging from several centuries at the start of Volume 1, dealing with early times, to six or seven years in Volumes 9 and 10, addressing the modern era.

In part, the difference reflects the fact that much more is known about recent times than about distant eras. Yet it also reflects a real acceleration in the number of noteworthy events, related to surging population growth. Demographers estimate that it was only in the early 19th century that world population reached one billion; at the start of the 21st century the figure is over six billion and rising, meaning that more people have lived in the past 200 years than in all the other epochs of history combined.

The subjects covered by the feature pages may be a major individual or a civilization. Some cover epoch-making events, while others address more general themes such as the development of types of technology. In each case the feature provides a clear overview of its subject to supplement its timeline entries, indicating its significance on the broader canvas of world history.

Facts at a Glance lists names and terms that may be unfamiliar or that deserve more explanation than can be provided in the timeline entries. Check these pages for quick reference on individuals, peoples, battles, or cultures, and also for explanations of words that are not clear.

The comprehensive index at the back of each book covers the entire set and will enable you to follow all references to a given subject across the ten volumes.

TIMELINE PAGES

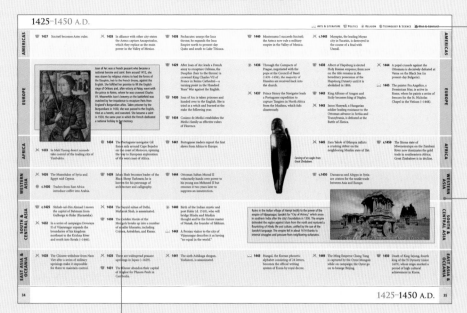

Symbols

Each entry is prefixed by one of five symbols—for example, crossed swords for war, an open book for arts and literature—indicating a particular category of history. A key to the symbols is printed at the top of the right-hand page.

Bands

Each timeline is divided into five or six bands relating to different continents or other major regions of the world. Within each band events are listed in chronological (time) order.

Boxes

Boxes in each timeline present more detailed information about important individuals, places, events, or works.

FEATURE PAGES

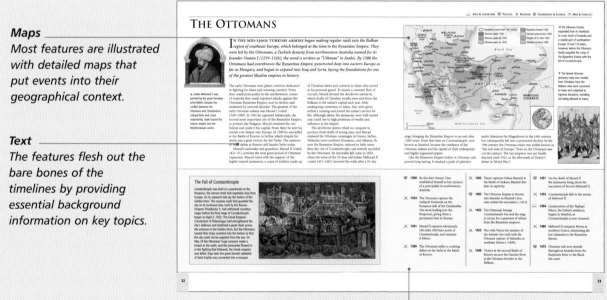

Maps

Most features are illustrated with detailed maps that put events into their geographical context.

Text

The features flesh out the bare bones of the timelines by providing essential background information on key topics.

Subject-specific timelines

Each feature has a timeline devoted exclusively to its topic to give an at-a-glance overview of the main developments in its history.

AMERICAS

1900 Republican William McKinley is reelected president of the United States, defeating radical challenger William Jennings Bryan for a second time.

1901 President McKinley is assassinated by an anarchist. Vice-President Theodore Roosevelt succeeds him.

1902 The British, German, and Italian navies act jointly to blockade Venezuelan ports over unpaid government debt.

EUROPE

1901 Britain's Queen Victoria dies, and is succeeded by her son Edward VII.

1903 In Britain Emmeline Pankhurst forms the Women's Social and Political Union to campaign for women's suffrage (the right to vote). Its supporters are known as suffragettes.

English suffragette leader Emmeline Pankhurst addresses a crowd in 1908.

1903 Russia's Social Democratic Party splits between the minority Mensheviks and the majority (and more extreme) Bolsheviks.

1904 Britain and France ally themselves in the Entente Cordiale ("Friendly Understanding").

AFRICA

1900 In the Second Boer War British armies relieve besieged British forces at Kimberley, Ladysmith, and Mafeking, South Africa.

1901 Ashanti in northern Nigeria is annexed to Britain's Gold Coast colony (later Ghana).

1903 Britain completes the conquest of northern Nigeria, ruling the region as a protectorate through the existing Sokoto Caliphate.

1904 Belgium appoints a commission to investigate oppression in the Congo Free State.

1904 The German authorities in South West Africa (now Namibia) suppress the Herero people, killing three-quarters of the population (–1907).

WESTERN ASIA

1901 The Zionist leader Theodor Herzl meets with Ottoman Sultan Abdul Hamid II, hoping to persuade him to grant land in Palestine for a Jewish state.

1901 Iran grants a 60-year monopoly on oil-exploitation rights through most of the country to William Knox D'Arcy, a British citizen.

1902 Abd al-Aziz ibn Sa'ud returns from exile to take Riyadh, creating the third Saudi state while still nominally acknowledging the ultimate authority of the Ottoman sultan.

SOUTH & CENTRAL ASIA

1904 Britain sends a force to Tibet on the pretext of protecting the country from Russian interference and compels Tibet to open its borders to foreign trade.

1905 Britain's viceroy in India, Lord Curzon, divides Bengal into a largely Hindu Western Bengal and a mainly Muslim Eastern Bengal and Assam.

1906 An Anglo-Chinese convention recognizes Chinese sovereignty over Tibet.

EAST ASIA & OCEANIA

1900 The Boxer Rebellion breaks out in China, marked by attacks on foreigners and their embassies. An international force including U.S., British, Russian, French, and Japanese contingents is brought in to put the rising down.

1900 Russian forces take control of Manchuria from China.

1901 An administration is set up in the U.S.-run Philippines. The United States backs the conservative Federal Party as popular resistance continues despite the capture of the rebel leader Emilio Aguinaldo.

1901 Various British colonies come together to form the Commonwealth of Australia.

As this cartoon showing the Japanese emperor taming the Russian bear suggests, Japan's victory over Russia in the Russo–Japanese War of 1904–1905 represented a significant shift in the global balance of power. For the first time in more than two centuries a European power was humiliatingly defeated by an Asian nation. Japan's success was a sign that the colonial order of the 19th century might be coming to an end. It also encouraged militarism in Japan's ruling elite.

✕ **1902** Colombia's War of the Thousand Days comes to an end, with 100,000 people killed.

👑 **1903** When the French Panama Canal Company goes bust, the United States buys the lease of the Canal Zone and supports Panama's secession from Colombia as an independent nation.

✕ **1904** Civil war breaks out in Uruguay between the landowning Blancos and the urban, liberal Colorados.

⊛ **1906** An earthquake and ensuing fire devastate San Francisco.

AMERICAS

👑 **1905** Norway breaks away from union with Sweden, choosing Prince Carl of Denmark to reign as King Haakon VII.

✕ **1905** In St. Petersburg the czar's troops fire on demonstrating workers on Bloody Sunday, triggering a wider uprising. To quell the unrest, Nicholas II concedes limited reforms, including the establishment of an elected assembly, the duma.

👑 **1906** The first Labour Party members are elected to the British Parliament.

👑 **1906** Russia's duma meets for the first time, only to be quickly dissolved by the czar, who considers it too radical.

EUROPE

👑 **1906** By the Treaty of Algeciras European powers agree to recognize the claims of France and Spain to rule Morocco.

Beginning in 1899, the Second Boer War set farmers of Dutch origin (left) living in southern Africa against the British. It was an unequal contest that the British Army was always likely to win. Yet the Boers fought so well that the Treaty of Vereeniging, which ended the war in 1902, won them substantial concessions.

AFRICA

✕ **1903** Rioting stirred by resentment at foreign influence breaks out in the Iranian cities of Esfahan and Yazd, with violence directed against members of the Baha'i faith.

✕ **1904** A force sent to bolster Ottoman authority is defeated by Abd al-Aziz ibn Sa'ud, further boosting Saudi prestige in Arabia.

👑 **1906** In response to growing unrest, Shah Muzaffar ud-Din is forced to concede a constitution in Iran. A *majlis*, or constituent assembly, is established.

WESTERN ASIA

👑 **1906** The Simla Deputation, a body of leading Muslims, calls on the new viceroy of India, Lord Minto, to improve the status of India's Muslim minority.

👑 **1906** The All India Muslim League is founded as a mouthpiece for India's Islamic community

SOUTH & CENTRAL ASIA

✕ **1902** The Philippines insurrection is suppressed, but smaller scale resistance continues.

👑 **1902** Japan allies with Britain to resist Russian expansion in East Asia.

✕ **1904** The Russo–Japanese War breaks out.

✕ **1905** Japanese forces gain control of Manchuria and defeat the Russian Pacific fleet in the naval Battle of Tsushima.

👑 **1905** The Treaty of Portsmouth ends the Russo–Japanese War. Japan gains northern Sakhalin and is given a free hand to establish a protectorate in Korea.

EAST ASIA & OCEANIA

1900–1906 A.D.

7

AMERICAS

Members of the NAACP march in protest against lynchings.

⚔ **1907** Industrial unrest sweeps Chile.

👑 **1910** The National Association for the Advancement of Colored People (NAACP) is founded to campaign for the rights of African–Americans.

⚔ **1910** The Mexican Revolution breaks out when Francisco Madero is elected president but denied office. The dictatorship of Porfirio Díaz, who originally came to power in 1877, is subsequently overthrown (in 1911), and Madero installed in power.

EUROPE

👑 **1907** The Triple Entente among Britain, France, and Russia comes together to counter the Triple Alliance already formed by Germany, Austria-Hungary, and Italy.

👑 **1908** Crete takes advantage of Ottoman troubles to declare union with Greece.

👑 **1908** Bulgaria declares its independence from the Ottoman Empire.

✳ **1909** French aviator Louis Blériot makes the first powered flight across the English Channel.

👑 **1910** Revolution in Portugal: The monarchy is brought down and a republic proclaimed.

👑 **1910** George V ascends the British throne at a time when the British Empire is at its peak.

Louis Blériot arrives in England after completing the first cross-Channel flight.

AFRICA

👑 **1908** Belgium takes direct charge of the administration of the Congo Free State, which is renamed Belgian Congo.

👑 **1910** South Africa gains autonomy as an independent dominion of the British Empire. Afrikaner leader Louis Botha is elected prime minister in white-only elections.

👑 **1911** The Agadir Incident sees France and Germany squaring up over rival colonial claims to influence in Morocco.

WESTERN ASIA

👑 **1908** Young Turks stage a revolution in Ottoman Turkey, seeking to establish a constitutional government while keeping Sultan Abdul Hamid II as head of state.

👑 **1909** In Persia supporters of constitutional government depose Shah Muhammad Ali and place his young son Ahmad on the Iranian throne, with a regent.

👑 **1909** After the failure of a counter-revolutionary coup, Ottoman Sultan Abdul Hamid II is deposed to make way for his more malleable brother Mehmed V.

SOUTH & CENTRAL ASIA

👑 **1909** The Indian Councils Act concedes increased representation to native Indians in local government, but the growing nationalist movement is unimpressed.

👑 **1910** Lord Hardinge is appointed viceroy in India. One of his first moves (in 1911) will be to annul the partition of Bengal, a decision greeted triumphantly by Hindus.

👑 **1911** The purpose-built city of New Delhi becomes India's capital.

EAST ASIA & OCEANIA

⚔ **1907** Japanese moves to disband the Korean army cause a widespread revolt against Japanese rule.

👑 **1908** China's Emperor Dezong dies, followed days later by Dowager Empress Cixi, the power behind the throne for 30 years. Power passes to the boy-emperor Puyi.

⚔ **1910** Japan annexes Korea. Over 20,000 Koreans have died in the three-year fight for independence.

👑 **1911** Sun Yat-sen leads a full-scale nationalist revolution in China. The following year Emperor Puyi abdicates, and the Republic of China is established.

👑 **1913** Reformer Francis Harrison is appointed U.S. governor of the Philippines. He advocates independence for the islands and places Filipinos in positions of responsibility in the administration.

👑 **1911** The Triangle Shirtwaist fire, in the New York City factory of that name, kills 146 mainly female immigrant garment workers, highlighting bad working conditions in "sweatshops" at this time.

👑 **1912** Theodore Roosevelt breaks with the Republicans to lead his own Progressive Party.

✕ **1912** U.S. forces invade Nicaragua. The country will remain under U.S. occupation for 20 years.

👑 **1912** The Democrat challenger Woodrow Wilson wins the U.S. presidential election.

✕ **1913** Mexico's President Madero is deposed and murdered by members of the military; General Victoriano Huerta takes power.

AMERICAS

✕ **1912** The First Balkan War breaks out when Bulgaria, Greece, Serbia, and Montenegro join forces to win their independence from Ottoman Turkey, along with that of a new nation, Albania (–1913).

👑 **1913** The Home Rule Bill granting limited independence to Ireland is passed by Britain's House of Commons but rejected by the House of Lords.

Britain's King George V, shown in these patriotic vignettes with his wife Mary.

✕ **1913** The Second Balkan War breaks out. Serbia, Greece, Romania, and Turkey now unite against Bulgaria, which has set itself against Serbian claims to Macedonia. Bulgaria is beaten and the region repartitioned.

EUROPE

✕ **1911** Italy sends a force to occupy Tripoli, Libya.

👑 **1912** Using local unrest as a pretext, France imposes a protectorate on southern Morocco; the northern third of the country becomes a protectorate of Spain.

👑 **1913** The Native Land Act ratifies the existing segregation of races in South Africa, with black African farmers confined to the more marginal lands.

AFRICA

✕ **1911** The Ottoman Empire wages war unsuccessfully on Italy to protest the Italian annexation of Tripoli, an Ottoman territory in North Africa (–1912).

✕ **1913** Young Turks led by Enver Pasha stage a coup against the sultan's ministers following Ottoman reverses in the First Balkan War.

WESTERN ASIA

👑 **1912** Tibet and Mongolia both take advantage of the revolution in China to reclaim their independence, expelling Chinese officials.

👑 **1913** Yuan Shikhai, newly elected president of the Chinese Republic, acknowledges the independence of Tibet and the autonomy of Outer Mongolia.

SOUTH & CENTRAL ASIA

👑 **1913** Elected president of the Chinese Republic, Yuan Shikhai suspends the constitution and expels Sun Yat-sen's Kuomintang nationalists from the assembly.

The Chinese army, some of whose troops are seen marching at left, gave its support to nationalist forces opposing the national government in 1911. The last Manchu emperor, six-year-old Puyi, gave up the throne, ending more than 2,000 years of imperial rule.

EAST ASIA & OCEANIA

1907–1913 A.D.

THE TRANSPORTATION REVOLUTION

▲ Commuters—one masked against smog—flood from a Tokyo subway train. Mass transportation was largely a creation of the 20th century.

THE FIRST WORKABLE INTERNAL COMBUSTION *engine was built as early as 1876; the first powered airplane took off in the early years of the new century, in 1903. Their inventors are well known, but other transportation revolutionaries whose entrepreneurship was as remarkable as their engineering remain largely unsung. The impact of their innovations would be felt far beyond the realm of travel, with implications for every aspect of modern life.*

On December 17, 1903, Orville Wright became airborne over Kitty Hawk, North Carolina. His flight lasted only seconds and took him no more than 120 feet (36 m), but its importance was immediately apparent. To have built a powered flying machine fulfilled a dream that had haunted the collective imagination for centuries: Was there any future challenge human ingenuity could not meet?

Less immediately apparent was the eventual global impact of air travel, although there were clues in the fast-expanding influence of the automobile. The achievements of the early motor engineers may have been less spectacular than the Wright brothers' feat, but their effect on the age was more profound. Many years would pass before air travel became cheap enought for mass transportation, but the auto transformed the United States as early as the 1920s.

Without the internal combustion engine such developments would have been impossible, yet the transport revolution was not just a product of advances in engineering technology. At least as important were innovations in industrial organization. Henry Ford pioneered assembly-line manufacturing techniques that allowed quality and quantity to come

---

1876 Nicolaus Otto designs the world's first practicable internal combustion engine.

1885 Karl Benz, another German engineer, produces an improved model, while Otto's student Gottlieb Daimler develops the prototype for the modern auto engine.

1900 Germany's Count Ferdinand von Zeppelin designs a rigid airship powered by an internal combustion engine. Within a decade "zeppelins" are making scheduled passenger flights.

1903 The Wright Brothers, Wilbur and Orville, make the first manned, powered flight in a heavier-than-air craft at Kitty Hawk, North Carolina. Orville is the pilot, covering a distance of 120 ft (36 m).

1907 An Italian-built Itala wins a 10,000-mile (16,000-km) auto race from Beijing to Paris.

1908 Henry Ford introduces the assembly line for the manufacture of cars. His new Model T retails at under $1,000—an automobile for the middle classes.

1911 Airmail is established in England, India, and the United States.

1913 Ford's new factory at Highland Park, Michigan, marks the coming of age of mass production: By 1914 it is producing Model Ts at a rate of one every 40 seconds.

1914 World War I breaks out in Europe. The next four years' hostilities will see aircraft mobilized for bombing, reconnaissance, message-carrying, and other roles.

1919 The first transatlantic passenger flights are made.

1927 Charles Lindbergh makes the first solo transatlantic flight in *The Spirit of St. Louis.*

1927 Production of the Model T Ford ceases. Some 16 million have been built over 19 years.

1928 British aviation engineer Frank Whittle conceives the idea of the jet engine. It will take him nine years to produce a working model.

1937 The highly-publicized *Hindenburg* disaster, in which the German airship bursts into flames at its U.S. moorings killing 36 passengers, effectively brings the age of airship travel to an end.

1939 U.S. engineer Igor Sikorsky invents the modern helicopter.

1964 The first Japanese bullet train enters service between Tokyo and Osaka, traveling at speeds of up to 125 m.p.h. (200 km/h).

1970 The Boeing 747 wide-bodied passenger plane comes into service. Such "jumbo jets" will help reduce the cost of flying.

together for the first time. There was a revolution in marketing, too. The spread of car ownership in North America was significantly boosted by fresh advertising techniques making sophisticated use of new media such as mass-market newspapers and radio. The falling prices associated with mass production did much to make automobiles more affordable, but newly devised credit-purchase plans also helped spread the costs. Thousands of families were soon able to own a car: The sense of empowerment the acquisition gave them was remarkable.

Thanks both to its industrial and commercial might and to its vast extent, the United States quickly became the first truly motorized society. Auto ownership increased rapidly after World War I, boosted by better roads and also by more practical design; in the course of the 1920s the open-top bodies originally favored largely gave way to models with roofs. By the 1930s North America possessed 85 percent of the global stock of motor vehicles.

Following World War II, however, car ownership also spread rapidly in other developed economies. In 1958 there were 119 million cars in use around the globe; by 1974 the figure had soared to 303 million, and in 1991 it reached 591 million.

Air travel made its mark rather more slowly; the technological challenges to be surmounted to get large numbers of people airborne were greater, and for a time dirigible airships competed with airplanes for passenger traffic. In the years following World War II, however, aviation too became a form of international mass transportation, dramatically reducing long-haul journey times in a world that was increasingly being talked of as a "global village."

▲ Wilbur Wright flies a glider biplane that he designed with his brother Orville at Kitty Hawk, North Carolina, in 1902. Having attached an engine to the plane, the brothers would make the first powered flight at the same location in the following year.

Factory of the Future

In 1913 Henry Ford opened a purpose-built factory at Highland Park, Detroit. Its most immediately striking feature was its sheer size. Ford saw that everything, from steel to working space, was cheaper bought in bulk. More radical, however, was the assembly line he had devised. Each vehicle under construction moved slowly through the plant, parts being added in strict order by designated workers performing the same repetitive task on each new chassis as it passed. Labor was plentiful and therefore cheap: Workers had to be trained in their single, designated tasks but did not need the all-around experience and expertise of earlier master craftsmen. Between the economies of scale Ford's gigantic plant achieved and the advantages of mass production, his manufacturing methods drove finished prices inexorably down. Eventually a Model T would retail at around $300, a sum even modestly prosperous Americans could afford.

AMERICAS

⚙ **1914** The Panama Canal is opened, although frequent landslides will limit its usefulness in its early years.

👑 **1917** An earthqake destroys Guatemala City and opens the floodgates of opposition to the U.S.-backed regime of Manuel Estrada Cabrera.

⚔ **1917** The United States declares war on Germany. In all, some 2 million U.S. soldiers will travel to Europe to fight in World War I; 115,000 will be killed (–1918).

EUROPE

⚔ **1914** Archduke Franz Ferdinand, heir to the Austro-Hungarian throne, is shot dead by a Bosnian nationalist in Sarajevo.

⚔ **1914** World War I begins, setting the Central Powers—Germany, Italy, and Austria-Hungary—against Britain, France, and Russia.

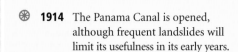

World War I led to the collapse of two empires (the Ottoman and the Austro-Hungarian) and helped end czarist rule in Russia. It also left 10 million combatants dead. Casualty rates were particularly high among infantrymen like these British troops seen going "over the top" at the Somme in 1916.

⚔ **1916** In Ireland the Easter Rising against British rule is suppressed by British troops.

⚔ **1916** British and German warships duel inconclusively in the Battle of Jutland, the major naval engagement of World War I.

⚔ **1917** Following battlefield defeat, Russia undergoes two separate revolutions. The first (in March) brings czarist rule to an end and establishes democratic government; the second, in November, brings the Bolsheviks to power.

AFRICA

⚔ **1914** British and German troops fight one another in Tanganyika. South Africa occupies German Southwest Africa (Namibia).

👑 **1916** Prince Ras Tafari seizes power in Ethiopia, toppling Emperor Lij Eyasu to rule as regent and imperial heir.

⚔ **1919** Britain exiles Egyptian nationalist leaders, sparking an uprising that is put down by force.

WESTERN ASIA

👑 **1914** When war breaks out in Europe, the Ottoman Empire allies with Germany and the Central Powers.

⚔ **1915** British and ANZAC (Australia and New Zealand Army Corps) troops land at Gallipoli in the Dardanelles but are beaten back by Ottoman forces.

⚔ **1915** Mass deportations of Armenians from eastern Turkey, intended to reduce the risk of rebellion, result in up to 1.5 million deaths.

SOUTH & CENTRAL ASIA

👑 **1915** Mohandas "Mahatma" Gandhi takes up the struggle for Indian independence.

⚔ **1916** Czarist forces put down an uprising in Uzbekistan against food shortages and poor conditions, killing thousands.

⚔ **1918** Soviet forces take Turkestan, triggering widespread (but uncoordinated) *basmachi* ("bandit") resistance by tribesmen across Central Asia.

EAST ASIA & OCEANIA

👑 **1914** A Constitutional Compact proclaimed in China confirms the dictatorial powers of Yuan Shikhai.

⚔ **1914** Japan joins the European allies in declaring war on Germany. It opens hostilities by occupying the islands of Micronesia, previously a German colony.

👑 **1914** Malaya is taken under British control.

👑 **1915** Yuan Shikhai announces his intention to rule China as a new emperor but dies (in 1916) before the imperial system can be restored.

🏛 **1919** President Woodrow Wilson's 14 Points peace plan is adopted at the Versailles Conference ending World War I, but the U.S. Congress rejects the treaty and refuses to join the League of Nations (–1920).

🏛 **1919** The Volstead Act (coming into force in 1920) bans alcohol and introduces the Prohibition era.

⚔ **1919** Peasant guerrilla leader Emiliano Zapata is treacherously killed amid continuing civil strife and disorder in the Mexican Republic.

🏛 **1918** British women over the age of 30 win the right to vote.

🏛 **1918** World War I ends in the defeat of Germany and its allies. The Austro-Hungarian Empire breaks up, and two new nations emerge: an independent Poland and the Kingdom of Serbs, Croats, and Slovenes (the future Yugoslavia).

🏛 **1919** The Treaty of Versailles imposes harsh peace terms on Germany, including the restoration of Alsace and Lorraine to France.

Vladimir Lenin led the Bolsheviks to power in Russia in November 1917.

🏛 **1919** The League of Nations is established as a forum for the resolution of future international disputes.

⚔ **1919** The Spartacists—German communists—stage an unsuccessful uprising in Berlin. In Hungary communists temporarily seize power under Béla Kun.

⚔ **1919** Civil war breaks out in Russia between the communist Red Army and counterrevolutionary Whites.

🏛 **1919** Britain takes over Tanganyika (Tanzania); German forces withdraw to Mozambique.

🏛 **1919** Upper Volta (now Burkina Faso) gains autonomy from French Sudan (Mali); Cameroon is split into French and British halves.

🏛 **1919** The Second Pan-African Congress holds meetings in London, Paris, and Lisbon.

⚔ **1916** Sharif Husein leads an Arab uprising against Ottoman rule. With British help Aqaba, Baghdad, and Damascus are captured (–1918).

🏛 **1917** In the Balfour Declaration Britain's foreign secretary declares his country's support for the establishment of a "national home for the Jewish people in Palestine."

🏛 **1918** The Ottoman authorities sue for peace at the end of World War I. Military defeat leads to the disintegration of the Ottoman Empire.

🏛 **1919** The British government passes the Rowlatt Acts, giving the authorities in India far-reaching emergency powers to tackle seditious activity.

⚔ **1919** British troops open fire on demonstrators in Amritsar, India, killing 379 unarmed protesters.

Yuan Shikhai, who became president of China following the revolution of 1911.

⚔ **1919** Nationalist discontent at the Paris Peace Conference's decision to restore German concessions in China finds expression in the Fourth of May Movement, sparking violent student protests in Beijing.

🏛 **1919** Ho Chi Minh founds the Indochinese Communist Party in the part of French Indochina that will eventually regain its independence as Vietnam.

AMERICAS

EUROPE

AFRICA

WESTERN ASIA

SOUTH & CENTRAL ASIA

EAST ASIA & OCEANIA

1914–1919 A.D.

AMERICAS

⚔ **1920** Mexican generals proclaim the Republic of Sonora, going on to defeat President Carranza and to force the surrender of the revolutionary leader Pancho Villa.

♛ **1920** The Nineteenth Amendment gives U.S. women the vote.

♛ **1921** Republican Warren Harding is sworn in as 29th president of the United States. One of his first significant steps is to raise customs barriers against European trade.

♛ **1921** The Immigration Act (further tightened in 1924) limits the number of foreign nationals who can enter the United States.

EUROPE

⚔ **1920** Admiral Nikolaus Horthy leads a counterrevolution in Hungary.

⚔ **1921** The communist Red Army finally overcomes its White opponents in the civil war that has divided Russia since 1918.

♛ **1921** Britain concedes autonomy to the Irish Free State, excluding six Ulster counties with a predominantly Protestant population; they remain part of the United Kingdom under the name of Northern Ireland.

⚔ **1922** The Union of Soviet Socialist Republics (USSR) is set up; Soviet troops occupy Ukraine.

⚔ **1922** Fascist leader Benito Mussolini leads the March on Rome, taking power as Italy's prime minister.

AFRICA

⚔ **1921** Spain seeks to extend its territories around Tangiers inland into the upland Rif region, sparking an uprising that also affects French Morocco.

♛ **1922** Muhammad Abd el-Krim, leader of the Rif Rebellion against French and Spanish rule, establishes the Rif Republic (–1926).

♛ **1922** Britain grants Egypt independence under King Fuad I but retains control over defense and foreign policy, the Suez Canal, and the administration of Sudan.

WESTERN ASIA

Shown here in the traditional clothing he later rejected for Western dress, Mustafa Kemal did more than anyone to create modern Turkey out of the ruins of the Ottoman Empire. From 1919 on he organized resistance to the nation's dismemberment, then oversaw the abolition of the sultanate and the establishment of a secular republic. He served as Turkey's president from 1923 until his death in 1938, winning from his countrymen the honorary title of Atatürk ("father of the Turks").

⚔ **1920** Greece attempts to divide Turkey in keeping with the terms of the Treaty of Sèvres, but Mustafa Kemal leads a successful resistance (–1922).

♛ **1922** Following the breakup of the Ottoman Empire, the League of Nations mandates Britain to govern Palestine and France to rule Syria and Lebanon.

SOUTH & CENTRAL ASIA

♛ **1920** The map of Central Asia is redrawn as areas in the former empire of the Russian czars are re-created as autonomous soviet socialist republics (ASSRs) of the Soviet Union.

♛ **1920** Gandhi's policy of nonviolent civil disobedience toward the British authorities is adopted by the Indian National Congress.

♛ **1922** Gandhi is arrested by the British on charges of sedition: He will spend the next two years in prison.

EAST ASIA & OCEANIA

♛ **1921** In Guangzhou (Canton) the warlords ruling much of northern China pledge to destroy the Kuomintang (nationalist) state; in Shanghai the Chinese Communist Party is formed.

♛ **1923** Sun Yat-sen reaches an agreement with the Chinese Communist Party: Kuomintang nationalists will fight alongside communists to free a reunited China from the warlords.

♛ **1925** Sun Yat-sen dies; he is succeeded as head of the Kuomintang by Chiang Kai-shek.

⚔ **1926** Chiang Kai-shek launches the Northern Expedition against the warlords.

AMERICAS

👑 **1923** Republican Calvin Coolidge succeeds as U.S. president on the sudden death of Warren Harding.

This falcon collar was one of the treasures found in Tutankhamen's tomb in 1922.

👑 **1924** The Coolidge administration is rocked by the Teapot Dome scandal, which forces the resignation of Secretary of the Interior Albert Fall.

👑 **1924** Native Americans are granted full U.S. citizenship.

EUROPE

👑 **1923** Hyperinflation devastates the German economy. French troops occupy the coal-mining Rühr region in response to the nation's failure to keep up with the war-reparation payments dictated by the Versailles peace treaty.

👑 **1924** Led by Prime Minister Ramsey MacDonald, the Labour Party comes to power in Britain for the first time.

👑 **1924** Lenin dies, unleashing a prolonged power struggle in the Soviet Union.

👑 **1925** Mussolini proclaims himself Il Duce ("The Leader") of a Fascist Italy.

AFRICA

📖 **1922** Pharaoh Tutankhamen's tomb is unearthed in Egypt.

👑 **1923** White colonists in Southern Rhodesia gain autonomy within the British Empire.

👑 **1923** Abyssinia (Ethiopia) is recognized as an independent state by the League of Nations.

👑 **1924** The Universal League for the Defense of the Black Race is founded in Paris by exiles from French West Africa. It will play a vital role in the growth of African independence movements.

WESTERN ASIA

👑 **1923** Kemal establishes a republic in Turkey with its capital at Ankara. Extensive measures are taken to westernize and secularize what had been a traditional Muslim society. The new nation receives international recognition in the Treaty of Lausanne.

✕ **1925** Having taken Mecca in the previous year, Saudi forces complete the conquest of Arabian territories previously ruled by Husein's Hashemite Dynasty.

👑 **1925** Iran's ruling assembly, the *majlis*, winds up the Qajar Dynasty, deposing Ahmad Shah and electing Reza Khan as first shah of the Pahlavi Dynasty.

✕ **1925** Druze tribesmen rise unsuccessfully against the French in Syria's Great Revolt.

✕ **1925** A revolt by Kurds in eastern Turkey is quickly put down, but Kemal takes advantage of the crisis to assume far-reaching emergency powers.

SOUTH & CENTRAL ASIA

👑 **1924** Soviet Central Asia is further redefined as smaller entities are subsumed into four socialist republics: Kazakhstan, Kirgizia, Turkmenistan, and Uzbekistan.

👑 **1924** The Mongolian People's Republic is founded; it will not be recognized by neighboring China for another 21 years.

EAST ASIA & OCEANIA

For 24 years until his final defeat by Mao Zedong's Communists, Chiang Kai-shek struggled for control of China. His Nationalist forces (left) battled warlords, leftists, and the Japanese before their eventual evacuation to Taiwan in 1949.

👑 **1926** Japan's Emperor Yoshihito dies. He is succeeded by his son Hirohito, who will reign until 1989.

1920–1926 A.D.

15

AMERICAS

Warner Bros. Supreme Triumph
AL JOLSON
THE JAZZ SINGER

Although not the first film to feature recorded sound, The Jazz Singer *marked the commercial breakthrough of "the talkies."*

1927 Al Jolson's *The Jazz Singer* inaugurates the era of "talking pictures" in the cinema.

1927 Charles Lindbergh makes the first nonstop solo flight across the Atlantic, flying from New York to Paris in his monoplane *The Spirit of St. Louis.*

1929 Republican Herbert Hoover becomes U.S. president.

1929 The Wall Street Crash: American shares lose more than $40 billion in value in a single month. The crash contributes to the beginning of the Great Depression of the 1930s.

1930 Revolution in Brazil brings dictatorial powers to Getúlio Vargas.

EUROPE

1927 Stalin emerges as the dominant figure in the collective leadership now ruling the Soviet Union.

1928 British scientist Alexander Fleming discovers penicillin.

1929 The Kingdom of Serbs, Croats, and Slovenes is renamed Yugoslavia.

1929 Stalin confirms his position as ruler of the Soviet Union by forcing his chief rival, Leon Trotsky, into exile. He launches the first five-year plan, aimed at modernizing the Soviet economy.

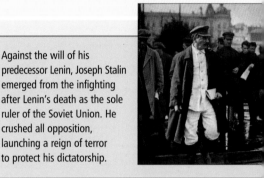

Against the will of his predecessor Lenin, Joseph Stalin emerged from the infighting after Lenin's death as the sole ruler of the Soviet Union. He crushed all opposition, launching a reign of terror to protect his dictatorship.

AFRICA

1928 In Egypt Hassan al-Banna founds the Muslim Brotherhood, an Islamic revivalist organization.

1929 The Riotous Assemblies Act is passed by the South African parliament to suppress protests by the country's black majority.

1930 Ras Tafari is crowned as Emperor Haile Selassie I of Ethiopia.

WESTERN ASIA

1928 On Mustafa Kemal's orders Latin script replaces Arabic for writing the Turkish language.

1928 France sets up an assembly in Syria but suspends it when it votes to end French rule.

1929 Fighting between Jews and Arabs in Palestine claims 250 lives.

SOUTH & CENTRAL ASIA

1929 Tajikistan—previously treated as part of Uzbekistan—becomes a separate Soviet republic.

1930 Leading Indian opposition to a salt tax, Mahatma Gandhi heads a march to the seashore at Dandi. He is arrested and imprisoned.

1931 The new viceroy of India, Lord Irwin, issues the Irwin Declaration, promising India a future role as a self-governing dominion of the British Empire.

EAST ASIA & OCEANIA

1927 Having defeated China's northern warlords, Chiang Kai-shek establishes a new capital at Nanking and orders a massacre of communists, his former allies.

1927 Ahmed Sukarno forms the Nationalist Party of Indonesia (NPI) to press for independence. His arrest by the Dutch colonial authorities two years later will cause widespread unrest

1928 Forced into flight by Chiang Kai-shek's purge, Chinese communist leaders Mao Zedong and Zhou Enlai succeed in establishing a Soviet-style statelet in Jiangxi, southern China.

1931 Japanese troops occupy Manchuria in northern China.

AMERICAS

⊛ **1931** The Empire State Building in New York City becomes the world's tallest building.

✕ **1932** Outbreak of the Chaco War between Bolivia and Paraguay, fought for possession of the disputed Northern Chaco region. Paraguay will emerge victorious three years later.

👑 **1932** In the United States the Great Depression is at its worst, with more than 15 million workers unemployed.

The Great Depression of the 1930s began in the United States but cast its shadow worldwide. The Wall Street Crash of 1929 led to an enduring financial crisis; eventually about half of U.S. banks failed. Lack of funds puts millions of people out of work; in 1932 alone nearly 20,000 businesses went bankrupt. Unemployed workers obtained what help they could from charity-run soup kitchens (left).

EUROPE

👑 **1930** Hitler's Nazis (National Socialists) run second in elections to the Reichstag (Germany's parliament), winning 107 seats.

👑 **1931** King Alfonso XIII leaves Spain as his country declares itself a republic.

👑 **1932** Stalin's attempt to impose the collectivization of agriculture produces famine in Ukraine.

👑 **1932** António Salazar comes to power in Portugal. His Estado Novo ("New State") dictatorship will rule the nation for the next 36 years.

⊛ **1932** English physicists John Cockroft and Ernest Walton first split the atom. In the same year James Chadwick discovers the neutron.

AFRICA

👑 **1930** The Land Apportionment Act sets aside the most productive half of Southern Rhodesia's land for white farmers.

👑 **1932** Upper Volta is subsumed into Côte d'Ivoire (Ivory Coast) in French West Africa.

WESTERN ASIA

👑 **1932** Iraq gains its independence under King Faisal I, but Britain retains a military presence in the country.

👑 **1932** King Saud's Kingdom of the Hejaz is renamed the Kingdom of Saudi Arabia.

⊛ **1932** Oil is discovered in Bahrain.

SOUTH & CENTRAL ASIA

👑 **1932** Imprisoned again, Gandhi goes on hunger strike on behalf of India's lowcaste untouchables.

EAST ASIA & OCEANIA

👑 **1932** A military coup in Siam ends 150 years of absolute monarchy: King Prajadhipok is forced to accept a constitution.

⊛ **1932** Sydney Harbor Bridge is completed in Australia.

Seen here under construction in 1930, Sydney Harbor Bridge had the largest single-arch span in the world when it was completed two years later.

1927–1932 A.D.

THE MASS MEDIA

THE RAPID GROWTH OF THE MASS MEDIA IN THE *20th century was in its way every bit as dramatic as the diffusion of printing 400 years earlier. The development of radio, television, and the movies created new audiences for entertainment and information. Advertisers were quick to grasp the power of these new means of communication in reaching out to a public of millions, and from the marriage of art and commerce the modern consumer society was born.*

▲ A rocket lands on a bemused Moon in a scene from one of the earliest fantasy films, George Méliès's *A Trip to the Moon* (1902). The first film shown to a paying public was exhibited in 1895; by the 1920s stars like Charlie Chaplin and Mary Pickford were famous around the world.

The early history of mass entertainment in the United States owes much to the inventive genius of Thomas Edison. He produced the first successful silent motion pictures, while his most famous invention, the phonograph, helped spread the popularity of ragtime, jazz, and blues music in the early decades of the 20th century. Piano sales fell as people listened to the latest sounds of Bessie Smith and Louis Armstrong on their wind-up gramophones.

Yet it was radio, which entered U.S. homes as a popular form of entertainment in the 1920s, that brought the greatest changes to people's lives. Sales of radios soared from a total of $60 million in 1922 to $426 million in 1929 as families tuned in to a diverse schedule of musical variety shows, comedies, and quizzes. Live broadcasts of baseball games and boxing bouts turned professional sports into a national obsession. At the same time, on-air commercials boosted the demand for new goods and products such as cars, refrigerators, and washing machines, and the soap opera was born when detergent companies began sponsoring serial dramas on radio.

Early experiments with television began in the 1900s, but it was not until the late 1920s that practical ways of transmitting television pictures were developed. By the mid-1930s RCA was transmitting television programs from Radio City, New York, and its regular broadcasting service was launched in 1939. But only around 200 TV sets were owned at this time

---

❋ **1895** The Lumière brothers open the world's first cinema in Paris, France.

❋ **1901** Italian radio pioneer Guglielmo Marconi transmits a radio signal across the Atlantic.

📖 **1903** Thomas Edison produces *The Great Train Robbery*, the first American commercial silent movie.

❋ **1920** The first radio news broadcast is made by Station 8MK in Detroit, Michigan.

❋ **1926** John Logie Baird gives the first practical demonstration of a television system in London, England.

📖 **1927** The first commercially successful talking film, *The Jazz Singer*, is released.

❋ **1928** Russian-born electronics pioneer Vladimir Zworykin patents the use of the cathode ray tube in televisions.

📖 **1935** *The Hit Parade* is aired for the first time on U.S. radio.

📖 **1938** Orson Welles's realistic radio production of a science-fiction story, *The War of the Worlds*, causes panic among American audiences.

👑 **1947** The Voice of America begins to transmit radio broadcasts into the Soviet Union.

👑 **1952** The first political advertisements appear on U.S. television during the presidential election contest between Dwight Eisenhower and Adlai Stevenson.

❋ **1952** The world's first pocket transistor radio is introduced.

❋ **1954** The first U.S. color television set goes on sale at a price of $1,175.

The Golden Age of Hollywood

In the early 1900s the home of the movie industry was New York, but by 1915 it had moved to Hollywood, whose clear California skies proved more suitable for filming than the uncertain climate of the East Coast. By the 1930s the cinema had outstripped all other forms of mass entertainment in popularity. In the anxious years of the Depression and World War II the world of the movies and the glamorous lifestyle of their stars offered audiences a heady mix of sophistication, passion, comedy, and swashbuckling adventure. The Hollywood studios at this time were making about 400 movies a year, watched by 90 million Americans a week. Hollywood's allure reached an early peak in 1939, the year in which two of the top-grossing films of all time, *The Wizard of Oz* and *Gone with the Wind* (right), reached the screens.

◀ A jubilant crowd in Washington D.C. holds up headlines proclaiming the end of World War I in 1918. News became a commodity with the spread of mass-circulation newspapers early in the 20th century.

worldwide, and television did not take off in a big way until the late 1940s and 1950s, when sets became cheaper, and programs such as *I Love Lucy* and *The Ed Sullivan Show* won large audiences nationwide.

News coverage was also radically affected by the new media. Advances in printing technology speeded up the flow of news to newspapers; but as the century went on, their monopoly on reporting current events fell, first to radio news broadcasts and then also to television and the Internet.

By the 1960s television was a major influence on American life. Broadcasts from Vietnam and images of the bodies of slain U.S. soldiers being brought home in body bags had a powerful effect in swinging public opinion against the war. More than 600 million people worldwide watched the first moon landing live on TV on July 20, 1969. From that time on world events, wherever they occurred, would be played out under the gaze of television cameras. A new age in global awareness had dawned.

⊛ **1962** Communications satellite *Telstar* relays the first live television transmissions around the world.

⊛ **1971** The first Internet e-mail is sent by computer engineer Ray Tomlinson.

⊛ **1989** Timothy Berners-Lee develops the worldwide web (–1991).

◀ Worldwide syndication turned some early TV personalities into international celebrities. Comedienne Lucille Ball became one of the world's best-known faces thanks to the global success of the sitcom *I Love Lucy* (left).

AMERICAS

1933 The Golden Gate Bridge is built in San Francisco Bay (–1937).

1933 Prohibition ends.

1934 After drought in the Midwest many farmers leave the "Dust Bowl."

1934 Lázaro Cárdenas becomes president of Mexico, introducing a program of social reform.

1935 Wallace Carothers develops nylon, a synthetic polymer, for Dupont; the first nylon product, a toothbrush, goes on sale in 1938.

1935 The Chaco War between Paraguay and Bolivia ends; the greater part of the disputed territory goes to Paraguay, but Bolivia gains access to the sea via the Paraguay River.

1936 The Hoover Dam is completed on the Colorado River.

EUROPE

1933 Adolf Hitler becomes chancellor of Germany; he assumes dictatorial powers and outlaws all political parties except the Nazi Party.

1934 Joseph Stalin eliminates political enemies in the Soviet Union; many are found guilty of invented crimes in "show trials" and shot, while millions more are deported to labor camps (gulags).

Adolf Hitler's Nazi Party came to power in Germany against a backdrop of economic breakdown and lingering bitterness over the nation's defeat in World War I. Although the party was voted in democratically, it rapidly set about outlawing democracy, taking all the reins of authority, both constitutional and judicial, into its own hands. Thereafter it based its actions on a racist ideology, an aggressive foreign policy at the expense of Germany's neighbors, and a totalitarian internal regime that subjected all citizens' individual interests to the greater good of the Nazi state.

AFRICA

1934 Libya is formed from the union of the two Italian colonies of Tripoli and Cyrenaica.

1935 An Italian army invades Abyssinia (Ethiopia).

1936 Emperor Haile Selassie goes into exile as Italy makes Abyssinia part of its African empire (–1941).

WESTERN ASIA

1934 Women win the right to vote in Turkey.

1935 Persia is renamed Iran.

1935 Mustafa Kemal is given the title Kemal Atatürk ("Father of the Turks") by the Turkish national assembly.

1936 British occupation authorities limit future Jewish immigration to Palestine following violent clashes with Arabs (–1939).

SOUTH & CENTRAL ASIA

1933 Mahatma Gandhi goes on hunger strike for Indian independence.

1935 The British Parliament passes the Government of India Act, introducing elected provincial governments in India.

1936 The National Congress Party scores convincingly in the first elections held under the terms of the Government of India Act (–1937).

EAST ASIA & OCEANIA

1933 Japan withdraws from the League of Nations.

1933 The Nissan Motor Company is founded in Tokyo, Japan.

1934 The Japanese install Puyi, the last emperor of China, as emperor of a newly created puppet state in Manchuria under the name of Kang De.

A woodcut by Li Hua symbolizes the agony of the Chinese people subjected to invasion by Japan.

⊕ **1939** Albert Einstein writes to President Roosevelt suggesting the United States should study the feasibility of a program to develop the atomic bomb.

Originally called Boulder Dam, the Hoover Dam was renamed in 1947 for the president who ordered its construction.

⚔ **1936** The Spanish Civil War breaks out between right-wing forces led by General Francisco Franco and the leftist Popular Front government. It will end in victory for Franco's forces (–1939).

📖 **1937** Pablo Picasso paints *Guernica* to protest the bombing of the Basque town of that name in the Spanish Civil War.

⚔ **1938** German troops take over Austria (March) and the Sudetenland region of Czechoslovakia (September).

⊕ **1938** German physicists Otto Hahn, Lise Meitner, and Fritz Strassman create nuclear fission (–1939).

⚔ **1939** The first Nazi concentration camp is established at Dachau in Germany.

👑 **1939** (March) The Axis powers—Italy and Germany—sign a formal treaty of cooperation, the "Pact of Steel."

👑 **1939** (August) Hitler and Stalin sign the German–Soviet Nonaggression Pact.

⚔ **1939** (September) Germany invades Poland; Britain and France declare war on Germany, beginning World War II.

👑 **1936** In South Africa black citizens win the right to vote, but only for white politicians.

⊕ **1938** A live coelacanth is caught off South Africa. The fish had been thought extinct for 60 million years.

👑 **1937** Turkey, Iraq, Iran, and Afghanistan sign a nonaggression pact establishing the Oriental Entente.

⊕ **1938** Oil reserves are discovered in Saudi Arabia.

👑 **1938** Death of Kemal Atatürk.

👑 **1938** A meeting between Gandhi and Ali Jinnah, leader of the Muslim League, fails to settle growing differences between the leaders of the Congress Party and India's Muslims.

Muhammad Ali Jinnah, leader of India's Muslim League, addresses a party convention in New Delhi.

⚔ **1934** Chinese communists break out from their enclave at Jiangxi, where they have been surrounded by Chiang Kai-shek's Kuomintang nationalist forces, and undertake the Long March to Yan'an in Shaanxi Province, where they regroup (–1935).

👑 **1935** Mao Zedong becomes leader of the Chinese Communist Party.

👑 **1936** Japan signs the Anti-Comintern Pact with Germany against Soviet Russia.

⚔ **1937** Japan invades China, bombing the Kuomintang-held cities of Shanghai and Nanking, and killing thousands of civilians. The ensuing Sino-Japanese War will last for eight years (–1945).

👑 **1939** The Kingdom of Siam is renamed Thailand.

AMERICAS

EUROPE

AFRICA

WESTERN ASIA

SOUTH & CENTRAL ASIA

EAST ASIA & OCEANIA

1933–1939 A.D.

21

1940–1945 A.D.

AMERICAS

1941 At a secret meeting off the coast of Newfoundland President Roosevelt and British leader Winston Churchill set out the terms of the Atlantic Charter for the future of postwar Europe.

1942 A team led by Italian physicist Enrico Fermi sets off the first controlled, self-sustaining nuclear chain reaction at Stagg Field, University of Chicago.

1945 President Roosevelt dies in office less than six months after becoming the only U.S. president in history to be reelected to a fourth term.

EUROPE

1940 (April–June) Germany invades and occupies Denmark, Norway, the Netherlands, and France.

1940 (June) French General Charles de Gaulle escapes to England and founds the Free French movement.

1940 (September) German planes bomb England in the Blitz (–1942).

1941 Germany invades the Soviet Union; the Germans advance to Moscow by December but are forced back by the cold weather.

1942 The Nazis adopt the "final solution," a genocide campaign aimed at the total extermination of the Jews; mass deportations to the death camps follow.

A Star of David of the type all Jews over age six were forced to wear in Nazi-occpied territories.

1942 Defeat at Stalingrad, Russia, ends further German expansion in the east (–1943).

1943 (May) The Nazis suppress a Jewish uprising in the Warsaw ghetto in Poland.

1943 (June) Allied forces land in Italy.

1943 (July-August) The Battle of Kursk, the biggest tank battle in history, ends in a narrow victory for the Soviet army and leads to the collapse of the German offensive in Russia.

AFRICA

1940 An Italian attempt to invade Egypt from Libya is driven back by British and Australian forces.

1941 Italy surrenders its East African empire (Ethiopia, Eritrea, and Somaliland).

WESTERN ASIA

1941 A joint British–Soviet force invades and occupies Iran, which is sympathetic to Germany (–1942).

1943 Lebanon gains independence from France.

1945 The Arab League is founded with seven initial members; it aims to speak for all Arab nations.

SOUTH & CENTRAL ASIA

1940 The Muslim League, meeting at Lahore, demands that those regions in which Muslims are the majority population should become independent states within India.

1942 Japanese troops advancing through Burma (Myanmar) reach the border with India.

1943 Indian nationalist leader Subhas Chandra Bose, fighting against the British in Burma, announces the formation of a Provisional Government of Free India.

EAST ASIA & OCEANIA

1940 Japan occupies French Indochina, the Philippines, the Dutch East Indies, Malaya, and Singapore, which falls in February 1942.

1941 The Japanese navy launches a surprise attack on the U.S. fleet in Pearl Harbor, Hawaii.

The Japanese attack on Pearl Harbor on December 7, 1941, killed over 2,000 people and sank 29 ships.

1942 U.S. forces begin to make significant gains in the war against Japan after defeating the Japanese fleet at the Battle of Midway (June) and landing on Guadalcanal in the Solomon Islands (August).

1944 (July) Hideki Tojo resigns as prime minister of Japan as U.S. forces continues to make gains in the Pacific.

⊛ **1945** The first atomic bomb is detonated in the desert near Los Alamos, New Mexico, by scientists working on the Manhattan Project.

👑 **1945** Mass demonstrations on behalf of jailed populist Argentinian leader Juan Perón bring about his release and propel him into the presidency (in 1946).

👑 **1945** The United Nations charter, drawn up at the Dumbarton Oaks Conference in Washington, D.C., in 1944, is signed at the San Francisco Conference.

World War II saw the United States allied with the democratic nations of Western Europe and with the Soviet Union against Hitler's Germany, Mussolini's Italy, and the militarist government of Japan. In the west victory in North Africa in 1943 was followed by the liberation of Italy (1943–1944) and the post-D-Day drive through France into Germany (1944–1945). The war in the Pacific theater was marked by initial gains by Japan, whose forces were gradually driven back by troops such as the Marines shown planting the U.S. flag on Iwo Jima in February 1945 (right).

✗ **1944** On D-Day (June 6) Allied troops commanded by General Dwight D. Eisenhower land in Normandy, France, at the start of the campaign to liberate Europe.

✗ **1945** Hitler commits suicide as the Soviet Red Army approaches Berlin.

👑 **1945** Germany surrenders on May 7, ending the war in Europe; the next day, May 8, is celebrated as VE (Victory in Europe) Day.

✗ **1941** The German Afrika Korps regains land in North Africa until checked at El Alamein (1942).

✗ **1942** An Anglo–American force under General Dwight D. Eisenhower invades French North Africa.

✗ **1943** Axis resistance in North Africa comes to an end by mid-May.

✗ **1945** Jewish militant groups resume attacks against British military targets in Palestine.

👑 **1944** Gandhi launches the "Quit India" campaign, demanding Britain's immediate withdrawal; he is arrested and held in prison for two years.

👑 **1945** Britain releases Indian nationalist leaders from prison.

✗ **1944** (December) The Japanese use kamikaze pilots at the Battle of Leyte Gulf in the Philippines, the largest naval battle in history and a major U.S. victory.

✗ **1945** One month after atomic bombs are dropped on Hiroshima and Nagasaki, U.S. General Douglas MacArthur and Admiral Chester Nimitz accept the surrender of Japan on board USS *Missouri*.

The dropping of atomic bombs on the Japanese cities of Hiroshima and Nagasaki in August 1945 introduced a new era of mass destruction on a potentially devastating scale. The awesome power of the weapons raised the specter of widespread annihilation, fundamentally changing the nature of war.

AMERICAS

EUROPE

AFRICA

WESTERN ASIA

SOUTH & CENTRAL ASIA

EAST ASIA & OCEANIA

1946-1952 A.D.

AMERICAS

1947 President Harry S. Truman commits the United States to support free peoples in the struggle against communist totalitarianism (the "Truman Doctrine"); immediate aid is given to Greece and Turkey.

1947 Secretary of State George Marshall announces a plan to help Europe rebuild its war-shattered economies (the Marshall Plan).

Chuck Yeager pilots the record-breaking Bell X-1.

1947 Chuck Yeager becomes the first man to break the sound barrier, flying a Bell X-1.

EUROPE

1946 Italy becomes a republic after a referendum decides in favor of abolishing the monarchy.

1948 Britain's Labour Government introduces a free, tax-financed National Health Service.

1949 Two separate states are formed in Germany: the democratic Federal Republic of Germany (West Germany) and the communist People's Republic of Germany (East Germany).

1949 The civil war (since 1944) between communists and monarchists in Greece ends in victory for the monarchists.

1949 The Soviet Union tests its first atomic bomb.

AFRICA

1948 The Afrikaner-dominated National Party wins power in South Africa.

1949 The National Party introduces apartheid, separating white from black South Africans, who are deprived of democratic rights.

1952 The Mau Mau uprising against British colonial rule in Kenya leads to a state of emergency (–1956).

WESTERN ASIA

On May 14, 1948, David Ben-Gurion proclaimed the creation of Israel (left). The Jewish state was bitterly opposed by Palestinian Arabs, who received military support from Syria, Jordan, Egypt, and Lebanon. Israel won the ensuing war, substantially enlarging its territory but creating an enduring refugee problem

1946 Syria and Transjordan win independence, respectively, from France and Britain.

1946 Jewish militants plant a bomb in the King David Hotel in Jerusalem, killing 91 people.

SOUTH & CENTRAL ASIA

1946 Jawaharlal Nehru is elected leader of the Congress Party in India as independence talks resume.

1946 Growing violence between Hindus and Muslims increases pressure on the British to create a separate Muslim state (Pakistan).

1947 India and Pakistan separate. Violence mars partition; 14 million people move between the two countries, and at least half a million are killed en route.

EAST ASIA & OCEANIA

1946 Women are given the vote in Japan.

1946 The Republic of the Philippines is formally inaugurated as an independent nation.

1946 The United States begins nuclear weapons testing off Bikini Atoll in the Pacific Ocean.

1946 Japan's new constitution transfers sovereignty from the emperor to the people.

1948 Separate states are established in North and South Korea.

1948 Hyperinflation in China weakens the Kuomintang government, boosting support for the nationalists' communist rivals.

1949 The Netherlands recognizes the independence of Indonesia after a three-year war.

1949 Chinese communist leader Mao Zedong declares the establishment of the People's Republic of China.

1949 Chiang Kai-shek relocates China's Kuomintang government to the island of Taiwan (–1950).

1950 The Korean War begins between the communist North, aided by Chinese forces, and the South, backed by a U.S.-led United Nations force (–1953).

🌊 **1947** Congress's investigations into communist influence in the movie industry lead to the imprisonment of ten Hollywood screenwriters and directors who have refused to cooperate with the House Un-American Activities Committee.

🌊 **1948** The Organization of American States is formed to promote regional peace and security.

🌊 **1950** Senator Joseph McCarthy's claims of communist infiltration in the U.S. State Department start a wave of anticommunist hysteria.

🌊 **1952** The United Nations Building is completed in New York City.

AMERICAS

🌊 **1949** The North Atlantic Treaty Organization (NATO) is set up to defend Europe and North America from the threat of Soviet aggression.

🌊 **1951** France, West Germany, Italy, the Netherlands, Belgium, and Luxembourg form the European Coal and Steel Community, the prototype of the European Union.

Nazi war criminals on trial at Nuremberg, Germany; 12 are sentenced to death in 1946.

EUROPE

🌊 **1952** A group of army officers in Egypt overthrows the monarchy and establishes a republic.

🌊 **1952** With UN approval Ethiopia takes over the neighboring state of Eritrea.

AFRICA

🌊 **1947** The UN approves a plan to divide Palestine into a Jewish and an Arab state.

🌊 **1948** The Jewish state of Israel declares itself an independent nation.

✕ **1948** The first Arab–Israeli war leaves Israel with extended borders; more than 1 million Palestinians flee Israel in the aftermath of the war, while more than 250,000 Holocaust survivors arrive in Israel from Europe (–1949).

🌊 **1949** Transjordan annexes the West Bank and renames itself the Hashemite Kingdom of Jordan.

WESTERN ASIA

✕ **1948** Mahatma Gandhi is murdered by a Hindu extremist.

🌊 **1948** Ceylon (Sri Lanka) wins independence from Britain.

✕ **1948** India and Pakistan go to war over the frontier state of Kashmir (–1949).

✕ **1950** Chinese troops invade Tibet.

SOUTH & CENTRAL ASIA

Mao Zedong, leader of China's communists, proclaims the birth of the People's Republic of China on October 1, 1949. Communists and nationalists had vied for power in China since the 1920s, although their contest was temporarily suspended during the Japanese occupation of the country from 1937 to 1945. When civil war broke out again following Japan's defeat in World War II, the communists unexpectedly prevailed, forcing Chiang Kai-shek's nationalist forces to seek refuge on the island of Taiwan.

🌊 **1952** Japan officially regains its independence as the postwar U.S. occupation comes to an end.

⊕ **1952** The United States explodes a hydrogen bomb at Eniwetok Atoll in the Pacific.

EAST ASIA & OCEANIA

1946–1952 A.D.

THE END OF EUROPE'S EMPIRES

▲ A sailor joins Jamaicans celebrating their country's independence from Britain in the streets of the capital, Kingston, in August 1962.

AFTER 1945 THE COLONIAL POWERS *of Europe faced growing opposition to their rule. Nationalist pressures within the colonies to shed the old ties of empire won international backing from the United States and the United Nations, whose charter, adopted in 1945, recognized the right of all nations to choose their own government. The path to independence was violent and divisive for many countries, but by 1975 nearly all the former colonies of Asia, Africa, and the Caribbean had become fully self-governing.*

Between 1940 and 1945 most of the colonies in mainland and island Southeast Asia were occupied by Japan. At the end of the war European rubber planters, tea growers, traders, and administrators returned to their colonial possessions, expecting to pick up the threads of empire as they had been before the war. Instead, they encountered well-armed and organized nationalist movements, many of them communist inspired, that were determined to fight for self-rule. By 1949 the Dutch had been forced to abandon the Dutch East Indies, which became the independent nation of Indonesia. The French pulled

out of Vietnam and the rest of Indochina after a humiliating defeat at Dien Bien Phu in 1954, paving the way for a civil war between the communist north and noncommunist south of the country that escalated into the Vietnam War of the 1960s and 1970s. In Malaya British-backed forces became involved in a long struggle against the communists before the nation finally won independence in 1957.

Britain was the largest imperial power in 1945. Although it handed over control in southern Asia by 1948, granting independence to India, Pakistan, and Sri Lanka, it did not give up its colonies in other parts

▶ The decolonization process got under way in Asia at the end of World War II, notably with the granting of independence to India and Pakistan. By the 1950s the first African countries were also winning their freedom. The "wind of change," said by Britain's Prime Minister Harold Macmillan in 1960 to be sweeping the continent, subsequently became a gale: In the course of the decade more than 20 nations won the right to self-determination, leaving only a handful of territories still under colonial rule.

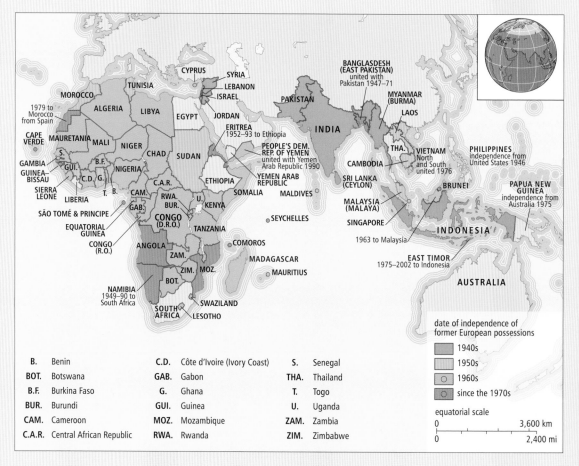

B.	Benin	C.D.	Côte d'Ivoire (Ivory Coast)	S.	Senegal
BOT.	Botswana	GAB.	Gabon	THA.	Thailand
B.F.	Burkina Faso	G.	Ghana	T.	Togo
BUR.	Burundi	GUI.	Guinea	U.	Uganda
CAM.	Cameroon	MOZ.	Mozambique	ZAM.	Zambia
C.A.R.	Central African Republic	RWA.	Rwanda	ZIM.	Zimbabwe

of the world so readily. Yet by the late 1950s it was obvious that the days of empire were over. In the 20 years after 1957, 34 new independent nations were created in the former British colonies of West and East Africa, the Caribbean, and the Pacific. In most the transition to self-rule was relatively peaceful. But the white settler community of Southern Rhodesia refused to hand power to the black majority, starting a conflict that lasted until 1980, when the country finally gained independence as Zimbabwe.

In French Algeria nationalist forces determined on self-rule launched a bitterly fought insurgency that plunged the French government into crisis in the late 1950s. Algeria eventually won its independence in 1962. Long nationalist wars were also fought in the Portuguese colonies of Angola and Mozambique, and the years of civil strife that followed the independence of the two countries in 1975 left them among the world's poorest nations. They were not alone in their deprivation, however: Most of the new countries of Africa lacked infrastructure and investment, and in the years following independence much of the continent experienced internal violence, dictatorship, poverty, and mounting debt—the harsh legacy of a century or more of colonial exploitation.

The Agony of Partition

In British-ruled India the nationalist struggle, led by Mahatma Gandhi, was well advanced by the outbreak of World War II in 1939. The war delayed progress, but in 1945 the British government began to prepare for the handover of power. In August 1947 India became two separate independent states: India, which was predominantly Hindu, and Pakistan, mainly Muslim. The partition was accompanied by terrible violence. Between 12 and 14 million people were made homeless as Hindus living on the Pakistani side of the new frontier fled to India, and Muslims journeyed the other way. There were mass killings too; historians estimate that between 500,000 and 1 million people were massacred as sectarian hatred reached heights not witnessed before in the subcontinent.

👑 **1946** French forces return to Indochina, newly liberated from Japanese control.

👑 **1946** The Philippines become independent of the United States.

👑 **1947** The independent states of India and Pakistan come into being.

👑 **1948** Ceylon (Sri Lanka) and Burma (Myanmar) gain their independence from Britain.

👑 **1951** Libya becomes the first colonial state in Africa to gain full independence.

⚔ **1954** The French are defeated at the Battle of Dien Bien Phu in North Vietnam and withdraw from colonial rule in Indochina.

👑 **1960** France's former colonies in Africa win independence, with the exception of Algeria.

👑 **1962** Jamaica and Trinidad are the first British colonies in the Caribbean to gain full independence.

👑 **1962** In Africa Algeria finally wins independence from France.

👑 **1965** British settlers in Southern Rhodesia declare unilateral independence rather than accept black majority rule.

👑 **1970** The British Pacific islands of Tonga and Fiji become independent.

👑 **1975** Portugal withdraws from its colonies in Africa.

⚔ **1976** Indonesia forcibly takes control of East Timor a year after its independence from Portugal.

👑 **1980** Following a lengthy guerrilla war, the white government of Southern Rhodesia accepts majority rule, and the nation becomes legally independent as Zimbabwe.

👑 **1990** Namibia (formerly Southwest Africa) is the last colony in Africa to gain independence.

◄ In comapny with his wife Winnie, Nelson Mandela celebrates his release from jail in 1990. Mandela, who had been imprisoned by the apartheid regime 27 years previously, subsequently negotiated an end to white-minority rule in South Africa and in 1994 became the country's first black president.

AMERICAS

1953 Dwight D. Eisenhower is inaugurated as U.S. president in succession to Harry S. Truman.

1953 Jonas Salk succeeds in developing a vaccine against polio.

1955 A military coup in Argentina deposes Juan Perón.

1955 In Montgomery, Alabama, Rosa Parks is arrested for violating race laws after refusing to give up her bus seat to a white man.

1956 Cuban revolutionary Fidel Castro launches a guerrilla campaign to overthrow the dictatorship of Fulgencio Batista.

1956 "In God We Trust" is adopted as the U.S. national motto.

EUROPE

1953 In Cambridge, England, James D. Watson of the United States and the English scientist Francis Crick announce the discovery of the chemical structure of DNA.

1953 On the death of Joseph Stalin Nikita Khrushchev becomes leader of the Soviet Union.

Francis Crick (right) and James D. Watson exhibit a partial model of a DNA molecule.

1955 The Allies end their postwar occupation of West Germany and Austria; West Germany joins NATO.

1955 The Soviet-dominated countries of Eastern Europe form the Warsaw Pact in opposition to NATO.

1956 The Soviet Union sends tanks into Hungary to put down an anticommunist uprising.

AFRICA

1954 Rebels organized by the F.L.N. (National Liberation Front) launch a war of independence against French rule in Algeria.

1956 Egypt's leader, Gamal Abdel Nasser, nationalizes the Suez Canal; in the ensuing Suez Crisis Britain and France send troops to Egypt, but international opinion forces them to withdraw.

1957 Ghana (formerly the Gold Coast) is the first British colony in Africa to gain independence.

1960 In Egypt construction starts on the Aswan High Dam (–1970).

1960 South African police fire on antiapartheid demonstrators in the black township of Sharpeville, killing 69 people.

WESTERN ASIA

1953 A CIA-backed coup in Iran deposes Mohammed Mossadegh's nationalist government and reinstates Reza Pahlavi as shah.

1956 During the Suez Crisis Israel invades the Sinai Peninsula.

1958 Iraq becomes a republic after the monarchy is overthrown in a military coup.

SOUTH & CENTRAL ASIA

1953 In the Himalayan Mountains New Zealander Edmund Hillary and Nepalese climber Tenzing Norgay complete the first successful ascent of the world's highest peak, Mount Everest.

1956 Pakistan becomes the first Islamic republic.

1958 Ayub Khan establishes a military dictatorship in Pakistan.

1958 The army takes power in Burma (Myanmar), independent from Britain since 1948.

1959 Ceylon's prime minister, Solomon Bandaranaike, is assassinated.

EAST ASIA & OCEANIA

1953 The Korean War ends; North and South Korea remain divided along the ceasefire line of the 38th parallel.

1954 Vietnam is divided between communist North Vietnam, ruled from Hanoi, and the noncommunist South, with its capital at Saigon.

1955 A meeting of newly independent African and Asian states at Bandung, Indonesia, commits itself to anticolonialism and neutrality between East and West.

〰 **1957** The governor of Arkansas calls out the National Guard to prevent black students from enrolling in high school in Little Rock.

⚙ **1958** The National Aeronautics and Space Administration (NASA) is created to lead the U.S. government's space program.

✕ **1959** Fidel Castro overthrows the Batista dictatorship and turns Cuba into a socialist state.

⚙ **1960** The U.S. Food and Drug Administration approves the sale of a birth-control pill.

AMERICAS

〰 **1957** The European Economic Community (EEC), later the European Union (EU), is created by the Treaty of Rome.

⚙ **1957** The Soviet Union launches Sputnik I, the first artificial satellite; the Space Race begins.

〰 **1958** Summoned back to power from retirement, General de Gaulle founds France's Fifth Republic.

The European Economic Community brought together nations that had been bitter rivals in the past and created the framework for a peaceful future. It had its roots in the European Coal and Steel Community, founded in 1951. At first there were just six members—West Germany, France, Italy, Belgium, the Netherlands, and Luxembourg. The organization, which changed its name to the European Community in 1967 and to the European Union in 1993, had 12 members by 1986 (see flag, left) and 25 following a further round of enlargement in 2004.

EUROPE

The war waged from 1954 to 1962 against the French authorities in Algeria was the bloodiest of all the anticolonial struggles of the decades after World War II. Algerian nationalist demands for independence were bitterly resisted by long-established French settlers and the army. Summoned from retirement to address the crisis, France's wartime hero General de Gaulle finally negotiated a settlement that, following a 1962 referendum, created an independent Algeria.

✕ **1960** The province of Katanga attempts to break away from the newly independent Republic of Congo, starting a bitter civil war.

〰 **1960** The independent state of Somalia is created from the former colonies of British and Italian Somaliland.

Completed in 1970, the Aswan High Dam brought Egypt's annual Nile flood under human control.

AFRICA

〰 **1958** Syria and Egypt form the United Arab Republic (–1961).

〰 **1960** Nazi fugitive Adolf Eichmann is captured by Israeli agents and flown to Israel to stand trial for wartime atrocities against Jews.

WESTERN ASIA

〰 **1959** Fleeing Chinese communist rule, the Dalai Lama, the spiritual and political leader of Tibet, seeks asylum in India, where he establishes a government in exile.

〰 **1960** Sirimavo Bandaranaike, widow of the assassinated prime minister of Ceylon (Sri Lanka), becomes the world's first elected female head of government.

SOUTH & CENTRAL ASIA

〰 **1958** In China Mao Zedong initiates the Great Leap Forward—a three-year plan for accelerated economic development that ends in disaster following bad harvests.

✕ **1959** Communist troops begin to infiltrate South Vietnam along the Ho Chi Minh Trail—a concealed forest route from North Vietnam.

⚙ **1959** An international treaty recognizes Antarctica as a scientific preserve and bans military activity there.

EAST ASIA & OCEANIA

1953–1960 A.D.

THE COLD WAR

▲ A communist-era poster solicits volunteers for the Red Army. At the end of World War II the armed forces of the Soviet Union were the largest in the world, with some 5 million soldiers under arms.

I N 1947, WHEN COMMUNISM WAS ON THE ADVANCE *in Europe and Asia, President Harry S. Truman pledged U.S. support for the free peoples of the world resisting subjugation by another power. The U.S. policy of containment embodied in the Truman Doctrine lay at the heart of the Cold War, the period of hostility between the United States and the Soviet Union and their respective allies that dominated international politics in the latter half of the 20th century.*

The Berlin Wall

At the end of World War II Berlin lay within the Soviet-occupied zone of Germany, but the city itself was divided into four sectors. East Berlin was controlled by the Soviets and West Berlin by three of the other wartime Allies—the United States, Britain, and France. Access between East and West Berlin was sealed off after communism was imposed in East Germany, but a steady stream of refugees found their way surreptitiously to the western sector. It was a dangerous and desperate measure; people caught fleeing were shot on sight. From August 1961 the East Germans closed off the escape routes altogether by building a barrier of concrete and barbed wire that ran through the heart of the city. The Berlin Wall remained the most powerful symbol of the Cold War era until November 1989, when the East German government suddenly opened its borders to the west. A jubilant crowd attacked the hated wall with pickaxes and crowbars, and it came down almost overnight.

1946 British Premier Winston Churchill uses the phrase "Iron Curtain" in a speech at Fulton, Missouri.

1947 The governments of Eastern Europe (Poland, Czechoslovakia, Hungary, Romania, and Bulgaria) come under growing Soviet influence.

1948 The Soviets blockade West Berlin in an attempt to expel the other Allied Powers; only a huge airlift of supplies from the West saves West Berlin from starvation (–1949).

1955 West Germany joins NATO; the Warsaw Pact is formed.

1960 Soviet missiles shoot down a U.S. U2 spy plane flying over the USSR; the pilot, Gary Powers, is captured and tried for espionage.

1962 In the Cuban Missile Crisis the world faces the threat of nuclear war until the Soviet Union withdraws its missiles from Cuba.

1972 U.S. President Richard M. Nixon and Soviet Premier Leonid Brezhnev sign the first Strategic Arms Limitation Treaty between the United States and the Soviet Union.

1975 At Helsinki, Finland, the Soviet Union promises to respect human rights in return for Western recognition of postwar boundaries in Eastern Europe.

1979 The Soviet invasion of Afghanistan worsens relations with the West; the United States boycotts the Moscow Olympic Games the following year.

1983 President Reagan announces the Strategic Defensive Initiative (the "Star Wars" program) to develop a defensive shield against incoming nuclear missiles.

1985 Mikhail Gorbachev comes to power in the Soviet Union, inaugurating a new policy of *glasnost* (openness) and *perestroika* (reconstruction).

1987 The United States and Soviet Union agree to limit intermediate nuclear weapons.

1989 The Berlin Wall comes down.

1991 The collapse of the Soviet regime in Russia marks the end of the Cold War.

The Soviet Union suffered terrible losses in World War II, and in the wake of Germany's eventual defeat its leader, Joseph Stalin, determined to create a buffer zone against future invasion from the west. He sought to do so by imposing one-party communist rule in the countries Soviet forces had liberated in Eastern Europe. Stalin went on to close the borders of the Soviet-zone nations, erecting what came to be known symbolically as the Iron Curtain. The creation of a communist state in the eastern half of Germany in 1949 was stark confirmation of a Soviet-dominated bloc in Eastern Europe. In the same year the Soviet Union first developed an atomic bomb.

To counter the growing threat of Soviet aggression, the United States and Western powers formed the North Atlantic Treaty Organization (NATO). When democratic West Germany joined NATO in 1955, the Soviet Union responded by setting up the Warsaw Pact, a military alliance of Soviet-dominated states. The Soviet Union also gave military and financial backing to many of the independence movements active around the world at the time in order to build up a sphere of influence to challenge that of the United States.

Over the next decades the superpowers stockpiled more and more nuclear weapons. By the 1960s each had enough to annihilate the other several times over,

a situation known as "mutually assured destruction," or MAD. The Cold War came closest to turning hot in 1962, when Soviet missiles were installed in Cuba, on America's doorstep. President Kennedy ordered their removal. For a time the world seemed poised on the brink of nuclear war until a U.S. naval blockade forced the Soviets to back down. The incident alarmed both sides enough for the two to agree to halt further nuclear tests. In 1969, in a further effort to reduce international tension, talks to limit strategic arms got under way. But relations between the two superpowers, blowing sometimes warm, sometimes cold, continued to dominate international politics throughout the 1970s and 1980s.

Eventually the economic dynamism of the United States decisively tipped the balance of power. While the Soviet economies stagnated in corruption and inefficiency, American prosperity went from strength to strength. Soviet planners came to realize that they could not match U.S. expenditures on defense or on technological advancement, and that a radical change of course was necessary. Their first hesitant steps to open up Soviet society unleashed a pent-up wave of dissent in the oppressed nations of the Soviet bloc. The sudden collapse of communism in Eastern Europe in 1989 finally sounded the deathknell of the old Soviet system and brought the Cold War to a close.

▲ U.S. President Ronald Reagan meets Soviet Premier Mikhail Gorbachev at a summit meeting in 1985. The pair oversaw a time of détente, or a thaw in relations, as the Cold War finally wound down.

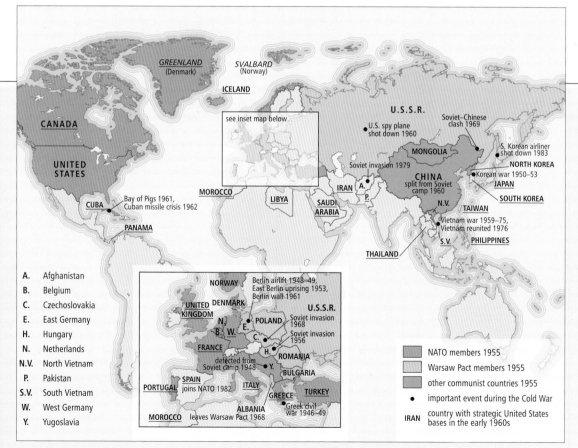

A. Afghanistan
B. Belgium
C. Czechoslovakia
E. East Germany
H. Hungary
N. Netherlands
N.V. North Vietnam
P. Pakistan
S.V. South Vietnam
W. West Germany
Y. Yugoslavia

◀ The Cold War divided much of Europe and Asia into two hostile camps—on the one hand, the democratic nations allied in the North Atlantic Treaty Organization (NATO), and on the other, the Soviet-bloc members of the Warsaw Pact. The situation was complicated by the presence of communist powers that were hostile to the Soviet Union, notably China, Mongolia, and Yugoslavia, all of which were fearful of Russian dominance.

1961–1967 A.D.

AMERICAS

1961 John F. Kennedy is inaugurated as the 35th U.S. president.

1961 The U.S.-backed Bay of Pigs invasion of Cuba ends in failure.

1961 Freedom Riders challenging segregation laws on interstate transport are attacked by angry mobs in Alabama and Mississippi.

1963 Martin Luther King delivers his "I have a dream" speech at the Lincoln Memorial during a civil rights march on Washington, D.C.

1963 President John F. Kennedy is assassinated in Dallas, Texas, and is succeeded by Vice President Lyndon B. Johnson.

1964 The Civil Rights Act opposing racial discrimination goes into law in the United States.

1965 Militant black leader Malcolm X is assassinated in New York City.

President Kennedy in Dallas shortly before his assassination.

EUROPE

1961 Soviet cosmonaut Yuri Gagarin becomes the first man in space.

1961 Russian ballet star Rudolf Nureyev requests asylum in France while performing with the Kirov Ballet.

1961 The nonaligned movement comes into being at a conference in Belgrade, Yugoslavia, hosted by President Tito.

1963 During a visit to Berlin U.S. President Kennedy emphasizes his support for the people of West Berlin, stating, "*Ich bin ein Berliner*" ("I am a citizen of Berlin").

AFRICA

1961 UN Secretary–General Dag Hammarskjöld is killed in an air crash while on a peace mission to Katanga, a secessionist region of the Congo.

1961 Independence wars begin in the Portuguese colonies of Angola and Mozambique.

1962 Algeria gains independence from France, with Ben Bella as its first prime minister (later president).

1963 The Organization of African Unity (OAU) is established in Addis Ababa, Ethiopia.

1964 Nelson Mandela is sentenced to life imprisonment in South Africa for sabotage and treason.

WESTERN ASIA

1961 In Israel former Nazi leader Adolf Eichmann is sentenced to death for crimes against humanity; he is hanged the following year.

1961 Kuwait becomes independent.

1964 The Palestine Liberation Organization (PLO) is founded.

1964 The Islamic cleric Ayatollah Khomeini is exiled from Iran for his criticism of the shah.

SOUTH & CENTRAL ASIA

1961 The Portuguese colony of Goa is united with the state of India.

1962 Chinese troops occupy the Aksai Chin region of Kashmir, provoking hostilities with India.

1962 General Ne Win seizes power in Burma (Myanmar) and imposes military rule.

1964 Jawaharlal Nehru, prime minister of India since independence, dies in office.

1965 Hindi becomes the official language of India.

1965 India and Pakistan go to war for a second time over Kashmir.

EAST ASIA & OCEANIA

1962 U.S. military advisers are sent to assist the South Vietnam government in its struggle against communist North Vietnam.

1963 China publicly criticizes the Soviet Union as a diplomatic rift opens up between the two principal communist powers.

1963 The Federation of Malaysia is set up, incorporating Malaya, North Borneo, Sabah, and Sarawak.

1967 Guerrilla leader Che Guevara is captured and killed in Bolivia.

1967 During a visit to Montreal, Canada, French President Charles de Gaulle declares his support for Quebec independence.

1967 Tens of thousands march in Washington, D.C., to protest the Vietnam War.

The civil rights movement of the early 1960s transformed the face of the United States. Demonstrators led by figures like Martin Luther King (seen center, left, leading a protest march in Washington in 1963) fought to end segregation in the Deep South and to fight discrimination throughout the nation. The drive for equal rights culminated in the Civil Rights Act of 1964 and the Voting Rights Act of 1965, which together gave federal agencies extra powers to enforce equal treatment of the races.

1964 Premier Nikita Khrushchev is ousted from power in the Soviet Union.

1966 France withdraws from NATO.

1967 British astronomers Antony Hewish and Jocelyn Bell discover pulsars.

1966 Kwame Nkrumah, first prime minister of Ghana, is overthrown while on a visit to Beijing.

1966 President Hendrik Verwoerd, a principal architect of apartheid, is assassinated in South Africa.

1967 Civil war splits Nigeria when the eastern province of Biafra attempts to break away (–1970).

1967 South African surgeon Christiaan Barnard carries out the first human heart-transplant operation.

A soldier on service in the Biafran War.

1967 Israel defeats its Arab neighbors in the Six-Day War, occupying the West Bank, Gaza Strip, Sinai Peninsula, and Golan Heights.

Indira Gandhi was part of a political dynasty: Both her father and her son Rajiv served, as she did, as India's prime minister. She served two terms in office before she was killed in 1984 by members of her Sikh bodyguard, angry that she had sent troops into the Golden Temple of Amritsar.

1966 Indira Gandhi, the daughter of India's first prime minister Jawaharlal Nehru, is herself elected prime minister.

1964 An alleged torpedo attack on two U.S. destroyers in the Gulf of Tonkin leads to U.S. entry into the Vietnam conflict.

1965 The war in Vietnam escalates as U.S. bombing of North Vietnam begins.

1965 Singapore declares its independence from Malaysia.

1966 Mao Zedong launches the Cultural Revolution in China (–1968).

1967 China explodes its first hydrogen bomb.

AMERICAS EUROPE AFRICA WESTERN ASIA SOUTH & CENTRAL ASIA EAST ASIA & OCEANIA

1961–1967 A.D.

1968–1974 A.D.

AMERICAS

1968 U.S. civil rights leader Martin Luther King is assassinated.

1968 Democratic presidential hopeful Robert Kennedy, brother of murdered President John F. Kennedy, is shot dead after a campaign rally in Los Angeles.

1969 Astronauts Neil Armstrong and Buzz Aldrin of the Apollo 11 mission become the first men to walk on the surface of the moon.

1970 The Boeing 747, the world's first wide-bodied airliner, enters service across the Atlantic.

1970 As opposition to the Vietnam War gains momentum in the United States, four student protestors are shot dead by the National Guard on the campus of Kent State University, Ohio.

EUROPE

1968 Student unrest spreads across Europe, protesting the Vietnam War and local grievances; students' and workers' strikes almost topple the French government.

1968 Alexander Dubcek's Czech government institutes the Prague Spring of liberal reforms, quickly crushed by Warsaw Pact troops.

1969 The Anglo-French Concorde supersonic airliner makes its maiden flight.

1969 In Northern Ireland violence between the majority Protestant community and demonstrators demanding enhanced civil rights for the Catholic minority sparks a 30-year period of "Troubles."

1970 Riots in Poland force the resignation of Communist Party head Wladyslaw Gomulka.

1971 Women win the right to vote in Switzerland, the last European country to introduce universal suffrage.

AFRICA

1969 Colonel Muammar al-Gadhafi overthrows the monarchy and proclaims himself Libya's leader.

1970 Biafra surrenders to Nigerian forces, giving up its three-year struggle for independence.

1971 President Mobutu renames the Congo Zaire.

WESTERN ASIA

1970 Civil war breaks out in Jordan when King Hussain expels guerrillas of the Palestine Liberation Organization, based in the country since their defeat by Israel in the 1967 Six Days' War.

1972 Three militants of the Japanese Red Army Faction carry out a machine-gun and grenade attack on the concourse of Lod Airport, Israel, killing 24 people.

1973 Egyptian, Syrian, Iraqi, and Jordanian forces launch a surprise attack on Israel while it celebrates the Yom Kippur religious festival; after initial setbacks the Israelis repel the invading armies.

SOUTH & CENTRAL ASIA

1971 East Pakistan rebels against being united with West Pakistan, 1,000 miles (1,600 km) away. East Pakistan wins independence as Bangladesh (–1972).

EAST ASIA & OCEANIA

The Vietnam War grew out of a civil conflict between the two halves of Vietnam established after the French withdrawal in 1954. Guerrillas from the communist North sought to subvert noncommunist South Vietnam, leading to the large-scale intervention of U.S. forces from 1964 on. Some 56,000 U.S. soldiers and 3 million Vietnamese died before the last troops were withdrawn in 1973. Two years later North Vietnamese forces entered the Southern capital of Saigon, reuniting the country under communist rule.

✗ **1973** With CIA help right-wing military forces under General Augusto Pinochet overthrow the elected Marxist regime in Chile; its leader, Salvador Allende, commits suicide.

👑 **1973** The former dictator of Argentina, Juan Perón, returns after 18 years in exile. Aged 77, he resumes the presidency as head of the Justicialista Party but dies the following year; his second wife, Isabel, will succeed him in power.

👑 **1974** U.S. President Richard M. Nixon resigns under threat of impeachment for authorizing illegal bugging of his political opponents at the Watergate complex in Washington, D.C.

AMERICAS

✗ **1972** At the Munich Olympics in Germany Palestinian terrorists from the Black September group kill two Israeli athletes and take nine others hostage; a bungled police rescue attempt results in their deaths.

The Concorde supersonic jet airliner remained in service until 2004.

👑 **1973** Britain, Denmark, and Ireland join the European Economic Community, increasing the membership from six to nine countries.

👑 **1974** A bloodless military coup in Portugal, led by General Antonio de Spinola, brings more than 40 years of dictatorship to an end.

EUROPE

👑 **1971** Idi Amin seizes power in Uganda, establishing one of Africa's most brutal dictatorships (–1979).

👑 **1974** President Habib Bourguiba of Tunisia is declared president for life.

👑 **1974** Ethiopia's long-term Emperor Haile Selassie I is deposed in a communist-led military coup.

AFRICA

👑 **1973** An international oil crisis takes hold as Arab oil producers curtail supplies to Western nations that supported Israel in the Yom Kippur War; the price of crude oil increases fourfold (–1974).

✗ **1974** To forestall a move by Greek Cypriots toward union (*enosis*) with Greece, Turkish troops invade northern Cyprus (mainly inhabited by Turkish Cypriots) and partition the island.

👑 **1974** The Arab League recognizes the PLO as the representsative body of the Palestinian people; PLO chairman Yasser Arafat addresses the UN General Assembly.

WESTERN ASIA

👑 **1972** Independent since 1948, Ceylon becomes a republic and changes its name to Sri Lanka.

👑 **1974** Floods and a devastating famine grip the fledgling state of Bangladesh, claiming hundreds of thousands of lives.

⊕ **1974** India announces that it has successfully tested its first atomic bomb, becoming the sixth nation to join the "nuclear club."

SOUTH & CENTRAL ASIA

✗ **1968** Vietcong insurgents launch the Tet offensive against South Vietnam, almost capturing the capital, Saigon, before being driven back.

👑 **1970** Fiji and Tonga win independence within the British Commonwealth.

👑 **1972** The South Pacific Forum is established to promote regional cooperation.

U.S. President Nixon visits the Great Wall of China.

✗ **1972** The United States begins unilateral withdrawal of its troops from Vietnam under President Nixon's "Peace with Honor" disengagement plan.

👑 **1972** President Nixon flies to Beijing to meet Premier Zhou Enlai, beginning a new era of rapprochement between the United States and communist China.

EAST ASIA & OCEANIA

1968–1974 A.D.

FIRST STEPS IN SPACE

▲ U.S. astronaut Buzz Aldrin steps onto the moon's surface on July 21, 1969. Neil Armstrong, his companion in the Apollo 11 lunar module, had preceded him a few minutes earlier, making the two the first humans to set foot on the moon.

THE IDEA OF VENTURING BEYOND THE BOUNDS *of Earth has long fired peoples' imaginations. The French writer Jules Verne described a fictional voyage to the moon as early as 1865, while England's H.G. Wells published* The War of the Worlds *in 1898. But science fiction became scientific fact in the late 1950s, as the United States and the Soviet Union competed against one another to take the lead in probing beyond the Earth's atmosphere. Within decades numerous missions had investigated most of the planets of the solar system, and some had traveled far beyond into deep space.*

Using the expertise of former German scientists who had developed sophisticated rocketry during World War II, the emerging superpowers built ever more powerful rockets, initially as ICBMs (intercontinental ballistic missiles) to carry their nuclear warheads and then from the late 1950s onward as space launch vehicles. The "Space Race" got under way in earnest in 1957 when, to the alarm of U.S. policymakers, the Soviet Union put the small Sputnik 1 satellite into orbit. Four years later the Russians scored another notable first by sending the first man into space.

American tethered "walks" outside space capsules caught the public attention in the mid-1960s, but the United States' long-term ambition announced by

President John F. Kennedy was to put the first man on the moon. This goal was realized on July 20, 1969, by the Apollo 11 mission—an event watched live on television by millions of people around the globe. In all, ten U.S. astronauts walked on the moon before the Apollo program was abandoned in 1972. Meanwhile the Soviet Union concentrated its efforts on unmanned probes to Venus.

In the 1970s and 1980s both countries constructed space stations: The Soviet Salyut 1 was launched in 1971 and America's Skylab two years later. Salyut was replaced by the larger Mir, which had a permanent crew, in 1986. By then a new era of space exploration had begun when in 1981 the United States embarked

---

✳ **1903** Russian physicist Konstantin Tsiolkovsky publishes *A Rocket into Cosmic Space*, in which he produces designs for multistage rockets and predicts exploration of the solar system.

✳ **1919** In *A Method of Reaching Extreme Altitudes* U.S. rocket pioneer Robert Goddard describes a project for a space probe to the moon.

✗ **1944** Scientists in Nazi Germany led by Wernher Von Braun develop the V2 rocket as a long-range weapon against the Allies.

✳ **1957** The world's first satellite, the 185-lb (84-kg) Sputnik 1, is launched by the Soviet Union; it orbits the Earth for 57 days, transmitting a radio signal.

✳ **1958** After several launch failures the first successful U.S. space probe is Explorer I, which discovers the Van Allen radiation belts around the Earth.

♛ **1961** U.S. President John F. Kennedy announces his country's intention of landing a man on the moon before the end of the decade.

✳ **1961** The first man in space is Soviet cosmonaut Yuri Gagarin, who makes a single orbit of the Earth in Vostok 1 before a successful reentry.

✳ **1962** Astronaut John Glenn becomes the first American in space, piloting his Friendship 7 capsule around the Earth.

✳ **1962** The U.S. Telstar 1, the first active communications satellite, goes operational, transmitting TV signals and telephone messages.

▲ Soviet cosmonaut Yuri Gagarin became the first space traveler when his craft Vostok I circled the Earth 188 miles (302 km) up in 1961.

✳ **1963** The Soviet Vostok 6 mission puts the first woman into space, cosmonaut Valentina Tereshkova.

✳ **1969** The Apollo 11 lunar module lands on the surface of the moon on July 21. Neil Armstrong and Buzz Aldrin become the first humans to set foot on extraterrestrial terrain.

on the space shuttle program, deploying reusable launch vehicles. The most notable shuttle mission took place in 1990 to launch the Hubble Space Telescope, which has provided clear images of distant galaxies. In addition, several deep space probes set off on long-term missions; almost 30 years after its launch Pioneer 10 was over 7 billion miles distant when it reestablished contact with Earth in 2001.

Heavy military and commercial funding sustained the huge cost of programs in the heyday of space exploration. One ambitious but ultimately unsuccessful venture was the U.S. plan known as the Strategic Defense Initiative (popularly called "Star Wars"), which sought to position laser-equipped satellites in space to target and destroy incoming nuclear missiles. The end of the Cold War saw state support for space programs greatly diminish, even though spy satellites continued to play an essential role in military surveillance. Yet pioneering work continues to be undertaken, and numerous satellites have been launched by the United States and Russia (and lately by China and the European Space Agency) to monitor weather, survey Earth's mineral resources, and further telecommunications.

◀ The Earth as seen from the space shuttle *Columbia* on a 1995 mission. Such images provided a new perspective on the planet, emphasizing its fragility as an island of life in space.

✳ **1972** The final moon mission takes place when Apollo 17 takes off from Cape Kennedy.

✳ **1981** The first reusable spacecraft, NASA's *Columbia* space shuttle, is launched.

✳ **1983** The Pioneer 10 space probe (launched in 1972) becomes the first spacecraft to leave Earth's solar system, journeying on into deep space.

✳ **1986** The space shuttle *Challenger* explodes shortly after blastoff, killing all seven astronauts aboard.

✳ **2003** The *Columbia* space shuttle breaks up on reentry over Texas, and all its crew perish.

The Saturn V Rocket

One key to the success of the U.S. Apollo program was the power and reliability of the rocketry employed. The largest operational launch vehicle ever built, the Saturn V rocket was developed by a team led by the German scientist Wernher Von Braun. Standing 363 feet (110 m) tall (60 ft/18m higher than the Statue of Liberty), these huge, three-stage rockets were equipped with five engines on each of their first two stages, generating some 7.5 million lb (3.4 million kg) of thrust. Only with such power at its disposal—used for a total of just 20 minutes—was NASA able to launch the heavy lunar module payloads beyond Earth's gravitational pull. A comparable Soviet rocket was a failure, and their moon program was abandoned. In all, 13 Saturn V rockets were launched without mishap. The enormous Vertical Assembly Building in which the stages were put together, one of the world's largest, still stands at Kennedy Space Center, Florida.

1975–1981 A.D.

AMERICAS

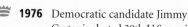 **1976** Democratic candidate Jimmy Carter is elected 39th U.S. president.

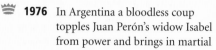 **1976** In Argentina a bloodless coup topples Juan Perón's widow Isabel from power and brings in martial law.

☀ **1978** In Jonestown, Guyana, 914 members of a religious cult run by the Reverend Jim Jones (including 260 children) commit suicide by taking poison.

✳ **1979** The United States experiences its worst nuclear accident to date when a reactor core at the Three Mile Island plant in Pennsylvania comes close to meltdown.

EUROPE

1975 General Francisco Franco, dictator of Spain since 1939, dies. The monarchy is restored under his chosen successor, Juan Carlos, grandson of Spain's last king, who sets about reintroducing democratic politics.

1977 Czech dissidents found the prodemocracy Charter 77 reform movement, one of the first organizations to openly challenge communist authority.

Members of the Solidarity union demonstrate in Warsaw.

AFRICA

1975 Portugal grants its African colonies of Angola and Mozambique independence; civil war immediately breaks out in Angola.

✗ **1976** King Hassan II of Morocco invades the Western Sahara. His troops are opposed by Polisario Front guerrillas supported by Algeria (–1992).

✗ **1976** Protests against the apartheid South African regime break out in the black township of Soweto, near Johannesburg; police kill 176 demonstrators.

WESTERN ASIA

✗ **1975** Civil war breaks out in Lebanon between Christian Falangist militias and Muslim forces supported by PLO guerrillas (–1991).

✗ **1978** Israeli forces intervene in the Lebanese civil war, bombarding the ports of Tyre and Sidon; a UN peacekeeping force is established in southern Lebanon to prevent insurgency against Israel.

1979 Egypt and Israel conclude the Camp David accord, a peace deal that brings an Israeli withdrawl from the Sinai Peninsula and promises autonomy to the Palestinian occupants of the West Bank.

SOUTH & CENTRAL ASIA

1975 Mujibur Rahman, Bangladesh's premier since independence, is deposed and murdered in a coup.

1975 India undergoes a crisis when a court calls for the resignation of premier Indira Gandhi; rejecting the demand, she assumes repressive special powers.

1977 A coalition of opposition parties led by Moraji Desai defeats Indira Gandhi's Congress Party in the Indian elections.

1979 Amid growing civil unrest and economic instability Shah Reza Pahlavi, who has ruled Iran since 1941, is forced to step down; the Muslim religious leader Ayatollah Ruhollah Khomeini returns from exile to set up an Islamic state.

EAST ASIA & OCEANIA

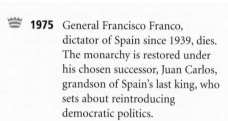

Pol Pot's Khmer Rouge regime launched a ruthless campaign of agrarian socialism in Cambodia (renamed Democratic Kampuchea). Most of the urban population was resettled in rural forced-labor camps. People whose loyalty was suspect—in practice, much of the middle class—were ruthlessly exterminated in unmarked killing fields (left). One-fifth of the population may have died in this way.

✗ **1975** North Vietnamese troops enter the South Vietnamese capital of Saigon, reuniting the country under communist rule.

✗ **1975** The Khmer Rouge gain control of Cambodia, launching a purge of the professional class that will kill between one and three million people (–1978).

👑 **1979** Nicaraguan dictator Anastasio Somoza is overthrown after a sustained guerrilla campaign by left-wing Sandinista rebels.

👑 **1980** Former Hollywood actor Ronald Reagan defeats Jimmy Carter in the race for the White House; Carter's reelection chances are seriously damaged by the disastrous failure of a mission to rescue U.S. hostages held in Iran.

⊕ **1981** The space shuttle *Columbia* embarks on its maiden mission from Cape Kennedy, Florida.

⊕ **1981** The first cases of AIDS (acquired immune deficiency syndrome) are diagnosed in the United States.

AMERICAS

👑 **1979** Margaret Thatcher leads the Conservative Party to electoral victory, becoming Britain's first woman prime minister (–1990).

👑 **1980** President Tito of Yugoslavia dies.

👑 **1980** Polish workers led by Lech Walesa establish the independent Solidarity trade union; the organization will play a pioneering role in the downfall of communism in Eastern Europe.

👑 **1981** John Paul II (pope since 1978) is seriously injured by a gunman in St. Peter's Square, Rome.

EUROPE

✗ **1977** War breaks out between Somalia and Ethiopia over the disputed Ogaden region; Ethiopia, with Cuban and Russian aid, overruns the region the following year.

👑 **1979** Uganda's dictator Idi Amin is driven into exile.

👑 **1980** Zimbabwe gains its independence under Robert Mugabe.

👑 **1981** President Anwar el-Sadat of Egypt is assassinated by Islamic extremists opposed to the Camp David peace accord with Israel.

AFRICA

👑 **1980** A military coup suspends democracy in Turkey.

✗ **1980** The Iran–Iraq War develops from a border dispute between the two nations; it will last for eight years and costs over a million lives.

✗ **1981** Iraq's attempt to acquire nuclear power is thwarted when Israeli warplanes destroy a reactor under construction at Osirak.

WESTERN ASIA

The Iranian Revolution of 1979 marked an important swing against westernization in the Islamic world. Muhammad Reza Pahlavi, who had ruled Iran with U.S. support since 1941, was forced into exile in favor of Ayatollah Ruhollah Khomeini, a radical Shiite scholar who had earlier been exiled by the shah. Under Khomeini's influence the new regime introduced strict Islamic law and favored Muslim tradition over modernization.

👑 **1979** Radical Iranian students overrun the U.S. embassy in Tehran, taking 66 staff hostage and demanding the shah's extradition from the United States.

✗ **1979** Soviet forces invade Afghanistan; they will become bogged down in a nine-year guerrilla war.

SOUTH & CENTRAL ASIA

✗ **1975** Following the collapse of Portuguese colonial rule, East Timor declares independence but is quickly invaded by neighboring Indonesia (–1976).

⊕ **1976** In the worst recorded earthquake disaster in history 655,000 people are killed in Tangshan, northeastern China.

👑 **1976** Mao Zedong, China's leader since 1949, dies. In a sign that the nation is moving away from Maoism, the Gang of Four—a group of intellectuals who were leaders of the Cultural Revolution, among them Mao's wife—are arrested. Put on trial in 1980, they will be sentenced to lengthy jail terms.

✗ **1979** Vietnamese troops invade Cambodia, deposing Pol Pot; the defeated Khmer Rouge regime will undertake a guerrilla war against the new regime (–1992).

EAST ASIA & OCEANIA

1975–1981 A.D.

1982–1988 A.D.

AMERICAS

1982 Argentina and Britain go to war over sovereignty of the Falkland Islands (Malvinas) and South Georgia; the British forces prevail.

1983 U.S. Marines are sent to Grenada to reverse a leftist military coup.

1986 The space shuttle *Challenger* explodes on takeoff from Cape Kennedy, killing all seven crew.

1986 Pilots Dick Rutan and Jeana Yeager fly their experimental airplane *Voyager* nonstop around the world without refueling; the flight takes nine days.

1987 On Black Monday (October 19) stockmarkets in New York and then around the world experience a major crash, wiping billions of dollars off the value of shares.

EUROPE

The Cold War rapidly started to thaw after Mikhail Gorbachev came to power in the Soviet Union in 1985. He and U.S. President Ronald Reagan (left) embarked on a policy of détente that culminated in 1987 in an arms control treaty, the first to reduce existing stockpiles. Gorbachev's attempts to liberalize Soviet society released a pent-up pressure for change that ended by bringing down the communist system both in the Soviet Union itself and in its Eastern Bloc satellites.

1983 Buoyed by success in the Falklands War, Britain's Prime Minister Margaret Thatcher wins a landslide general election victory.

1985 Mikhail Gorbachev comes to power in the Soviet Union on the death of Konstantin Chernenko; Gorbachev adopts a reformist agenda based on *glasnost* (openness) and *perestroika* (reconstruction).

AFRICA

1984 A major famine strikes Ethiopia and Sudan in East Africa, claiming around 100,000 lives.

1985 Live Aid rock concerts, held in Philadelphia, London, Moscow, and Sydney, raise $60 million for African famine victims.

1986 Tripoli is attacked by U.S. warplanes flying from British bases in retaliation for Libyan leader Colonel Gadhafi's support for international terrorism.

WESTERN ASIA

1982 Israel sends troops into Lebanon, starting an occupation that lasts three years (–1985).

1982 Hundreds of unarmed Palestinians are killed when Israeli-backed Falangist militia attack the Sabra and Chatila camps in West Beirut.

1983 Suicide bombers drive truck bombs into the compounds of peacekeeping troops in Beirut, killing 241 U.S. marines and 58 French paratroopers.

1985 Palestinian terrorists hijack the Italian cruise ship *Achille Lauro*, killing one passenger.

1987 The Palestinian *intifada* ("uprising") against the Israeli occupation of the West Bank and Gaza gets underway.

SOUTH & CENTRAL ASIA

1983 On his return to the Philippines to fight for democracy, opposition leader Benigno Aquino is shot by an assailant at Manila airport; the government is suspected of having a part in the assassination.

1984 Indian troops storm the Golden Temple, a Sikh holy site at Amritsar, where armed militants seeking an independent Punjab ("Khalistan") have taken refuge; over 700 rebels are killed.

1984 Four months after the Golden Temple assault India's premier, Indira Gandhi, is assassinated by members of her Sikh bodyguard in revenge.

EAST ASIA & OCEANIA

1983 Premier Deng Xiaoping of China introduces economic reforms that will transform China's largely agricultural economy.

1983 The Labour Party under Prime Minister Bob Hawke is returned to power in the Australian general election.

1983 A Soviet fighter shoots down a South Korean Boeing 747 airliner that has strayed into Russian airspace, killing all 269 on board.

👑 **1987** The United States and the Soviet Union sign their first ever nuclear arms reduction treaty, covering the two countries' medium- and short-range arsenals.

The space shuttle Challenger explodes on takeoff from Cape Kennedy, Florida.

👑 **1988** Vice President George Bush is elected 41st president of the United States.

👑 **1988** The United States and Canada sign a comprehensive free trade agreement, becoming effective on January 1, 1989.

AMERICAS

👑 **1986** Spain and Portugal join the European Community, bringing the membership to 12 countries (Greece having joined in 1981).

👑 **1987** Margaret Thatcher leads the Conservative Party to a third successive victory, the first such achievement in 20th-century British politics.

✕ **1988** A U.S. airliner is destroyed by a terrorist bomb over the Scottish town of Lockerbie, killing 270 people; a Libyan agent will eventually be convicted of the outrage.

EUROPE

⊕ **1986** A nuclear reactor at Chernobyl in Ukraine explodes, killing 300 people and exposing large areas of Europe to radiation.

👑 **1987** An accord between rival leaders Robert Mugabe (ZANU-PF) and Joshua Nkomo (ZAPU) to amalgamate their parties makes Zimbabwe a one-party state.

Live Aid stars raise money for African famine victims at London's Wembley Stadium.

AFRICA

👑 **1988** A UN resolution brings the eight-year conflict between Iran and Iraq to an end.

✕ **1988** Iraqi forces use chemical weapons against the Kurdish town of Halabja, killing 4,000 civilians.

WESTERN ASIA

⊕ **1984** An accident at the Union Carbide chemical plant in Bhopal, northern India, releases a cloud of poisonous gas that kills almost 4,000 people and permanently blinds many others.

👑 **1986** President Ferdinand Marcos of the Philippines is deposed by a "people power" movement led by Corazon Aquino, widow of Benigno Aquino.

👑 **1988** Benazir Bhutto, daughter of the executed Pakistani leader Zulfikar Ali Bhutto, becomes the country's prime minister (–1990).

SOUTH & CENTRAL ASIA

👑 **1985** French agents in New Zealand blow up the *Rainbow Warrior*, a Greenpeace vessel protesting French nuclear tests in the Pacific.

👑 **1986** Martial law, first imposed in 1949, is finally lifted in Taiwan.

✕ **1987** Two military coups are staged on the Pacific island of Fiji.

EAST ASIA & OCEANIA

1982–1988 A.D.

THE COMPUTER AGE

STARTING AS A MACHINE THAT STORED *data or performed mathematical calculations, the computer has become an indispensable tool of the modern age that can process information for myriad different purposes. Present in most factories, offices, shops, and colleges, as well as in a majority of homes in the developed world, computers have revolutionized the way people work and play.*

▲ An early IBM personal computer illustrates the classic trinity of box, keyboard, and monitor, which (with the addition of a printer) introduced millions of people to home computing in the last two decades of the 20th century.

Developed in the 19th century, the precursors of modern computers were punched-card mechanical devices that could store and process data. One of the pioneers of this technology was the U.S. statistician Herman Hollerith, whose company later grew into IBM. Yet the development of the digital computer as we know it today had to await the invention of electronic components such as thermionic tubes and transistors. The early electronic machines, developed from the latter part of World War II on, were large and expensive, and remained the preserve of major business corporations and government departments. These mainframe computers carried out large-scale clerical and administrative tasks such as payroll processing and census analysis.

▲ Colossus, developed in England in World War II to help break German military codes, was the world's first electronic computer.

1801 French inventor Joseph-Marie Jacquard mechanizes weaving by making a loom controlled by a system of punched cards that lower and raise threads in the right sequence.

1822 English mathematician Charles Babbage creates his "difference engine" to calculate complex logarithms; his associate Ada Lovelace writes a program for his proposed "analytical engine," a prototype of the digital computer.

1890 Herman Hollerith uses an electrically driven punched-card reader to process the results of the U.S. census.

1931 U.S. inventor Vannevar Bush builds the first analog computing machine to use electronic components.

1943 The first fully electronic computer, Colossus 1, is developed at Bletchley Park, England; it is used to decipher German military codes.

1946 U.S. engineers J. Presper Eckert and John Mauchly complete ENIAC, the first general-purpose computer. They go on to develop UNIVAC, the first commercial digital computer using stored programs, which goes into use in 1951.

1965 Texas Instruments develop the first pocket calculator, the Pocketronic (marketed by Canon from 1970).

1971 The U.S. corporation Intel produces the world's first microprocessor, the 4004.

1975 Micro Instrumentation and Telemetry Systems (MITS) produces its pioneering home computer kit, the Altair 8800, which can be bought by mail order.

1976 The world's first supercomputer, the Cray 1, is built for use at the Los Alamos nuclear laboratory in New Mexico.

1976 Bill Gates and Paul Allen found Microsoft, a software producer that comes to dominate the market in operating systems and applications programs for personal computers.

1977 Apple Computer of California, run by Steven Jobs and Steve Wozniak, introduces the first mass-market personal computer in assembled form (the Apple II).

1981 IBM introduces its Personal Computer (PC).

1984 Apple introduces the Macintosh ("Mac"), a revolutionary personal computer that employs a mouse, icons, and the desktop graphical user interface.

1991 The worldwide web is made freely available, revolutionizing the flow of information on the Internet.

2000 A virus known as "I Love You," spreading via e-mail, affects millions of computers worldwide.

The information technology (IT) revolution that saw computer use and ownership spread dramatically began with the advent of the microprocessor, a complex silicon chip that could operate around a million times faster than the first vacuum tube computers. The tiny size and weight of this component enabled the development of the microcomputer for individual use. The personal computer (PC) was introduced by IBM in 1981. Smaller companies entered a rapidly expanding market, offering cheaper "clone" machines that could run first the MS-DOS disk-operating system and then, from 1985 on, Windows, both of them devised for the PC by Microsoft. Another household name, Apple Computer Inc., pioneered its own Mac operating system and graphical user interface. Growth in this area has been enormous; while just 25,000 enthusiasts had home computers in the United States in 1977, by 2001, 178 million American homes were equipped with a PC or Mac.

As software programs in fields such as games or desktop publishing have become more sophisticated, so processor speed and hard-drive storage size have increased. Another major factor driving personal computing has been the popularity of e-mail and the worldwide web (see box below). These channels of information and communication are used by millions worldwide daily and have transformed the way people do business and spend their leisure time.

At the opposite end of the modern computing spectrum supercomputers performing vast numbers of calculations per second are employed to analyze complex systems. Research fields in which these massively powerful machines are used include weather forecasting, nuclear physics, and astronomy.

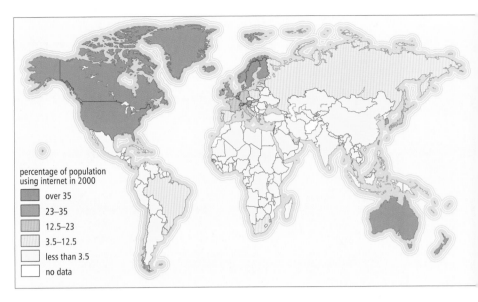

percentage of population using internet in 2000

- over 35
- 23–35
- 12.5–23
- 3.5–12.5
- less than 3.5
- no data

▲ By the turn of the millennium Internet use was most firmly entrenched in North America, parts of Europe, Japan, South Korea, Australia, and New Zealand.

The Worldwide Web

The worldwide web is a service that enables computer users to exchange information through servers attached to a network of networks (the Internet). It was developed in the late 1980s by a British physicist, Timothy Berners-Lee, who wanted to create a system for researchers to share documents and view each others' databases. With the growth in personal computer ownership the web took on a commercial dimension soon after it became freely available in 1991, with Internet service providers (ISPs) linking individual users to the Internet for a fee. The web is now home to millions of pages covering every conceivable subject, as well as countless companies conducting e-business online. People access it not just from their homes and offices but also from workstations in public libraries and in internet cafés like the one in Amsterdam seen at right.

1989–1994 A.D.

AMERICAS

🏛 **1989** Paraguayan dictator Alfredo Stroessner is ousted in a military coup after 34 years in power.

⚙ **1989** In the worst oil spill in U.S. history the tanker *Exxon Valdez* runs aground in Prince William Sound, Alaska, with devastating consequences for marine life.

⚔ **1989** U.S. troops are sent to Panama to topple its dictator, General Manuel Noriega, who is accused of drug trafficking and money laundering.

⚙ **1990** The Human Genome Project is launched with biologist James D. Watson at its helm; the base sequence of the human genome will be plotted by 2003.

🏛 **1990** General Pinochet steps down as military ruler of Chile, restoring civilian rule after 17 years.

EUROPE

🏛 **1989** Across Europe the communist regimes of Soviet satellite countries (Czechoslovakia, East Germany, Poland) collapse as their citizens demand democratic reform.

🏛 **1989** In Romania communist dictator Nicolae Ceaucescu is deposed and executed.

Demonstrators in Germany's capital celebrate the destruction in 1989 of the Berlin Wall.

🏛 **1990** Boris Yeltsin becomes the first freely elected president of Russia.

🏛 **1990** Unrest breaks out in some Soviet republics; Lithuania declares its independence, and Russian troops kill nationalist protestors in Tbilisi, Georgia.

🏛 **1990** East and West Germany are reunited after 45 years of division.

AFRICA

🏛 **1990** After 27 years in jail veteran South African antiapartheid leader Nelson Mandela is freed from detention, vowing to continue the struggle for black majority rule.

🏛 **1991** Kenneth Kaunda, leader of Zambia since its independence in 1964, is defeated by Frederick Chiluba in a landslide election victory.

WESTERN ASIA

📖 **1989** Ayatollah Khomeini of Iran issues a death sentence (*fatwa*) against British writer Salman Rushdie, whose novel *The Satanic Verses* is thought to insult Islam.

🏛 **1990** Over 1,400 Muslims die in a stampede during the annual pilgrimage (*hajj*) to Mecca.

⚔ **1990** Iraq invades the neighboring state of Kuwait; a UN resolution demands Iraqi withdrawal.

⚔ **1991** A U.S.-led coalition of forces under a UN mandate undertakes to liberate Kuwait; Iraqi forces crumble in the ensuing Gulf War.

🏛 **1993** Israeli Premier Yitzhak Rabin and Palestinian leader Yasser Arafat sign a U.S.-brokered peace deal; the PLO and Israel recognize each other's legitimacy.

SOUTH & CENTRAL ASIA

⚔ **1989** Soviet troops withdraw from Afghanistan having failed to pacify the *mujaheddin* Islamic resistance.

🏛 **1990** Benazir Bhutto is relieved of her post as prime minister of Pakistan after being accused of corruption.

🏛 **1991** A cyclone sweeps across Bangladesh, killing some 135,000 people and leaving millions homeless.

EAST ASIA & OCEANIA

🏛 **1989** Emperor Hirohito of Japan dies after 62 years on the throne; he is succeeded by Crown Prince Akihito.

Students in Tiananmen Square, Beijing, call for democratic reform.

🏛 **1989** Chinese students occupy Tiananmen Square in Beijing for two months, demanding democratic reforms; the protest is crushed by the army and militia.

⊕ **1990** The Hubble Space Telescope is launched from the space shuttle *Discovery*, although a flaw in its mirrors initially impairs its performance (repaired 1993).

👑 **1993** Bill Clinton becomes the 42nd U.S. president.

Saturn as seen from the Hubble Space Telescope.

👑 **1993** In the first Islamic terror bombing in the United States an explosion rocks the World Trade Center in New York.

👑 **1994** The North American Free Trade Agreement (NAFTA) links the United States, Canada, and Mexico in an enlarged free-trade zone.

👑 **1990** Margaret Thatcher quits as British prime minister after 11 years.

👑 **1991** The Soviet Union and the Warsaw Pact are both formally dissolved.

✗ **1991** The Yugoslav federation starts to disintegrate as Slovenia and Croatia declare independence; Serbian forces attack Bosnia when it too votes to break away.

👑 **1993** Czechoslovakia separates into two states, the Czech Republic and Slovakia, after a peaceful plebiscite approves this "Velvet Revolution."

👑 **1993** Nations of the European Community (now renamed the European Union) sign the Maastricht Treaty, committing them to a program of ever closer union.

👑 **1993** An attempted coup in Moscow is put down after President Boris Yeltsin rallies troops loyal to the reformist regime.

⊕ **1994** The Channel Tunnel is opened, linking Britain and France.

✗ **1992** A UN peacekeeping mission to Somalia ends in conflict between U.S. forces and troops loyal to warlord General Aideed (–1995).

✗ **1994** In the central African state of Rwanda interethnic violence between the majority Hutu population and the minority Tutsis claims over 1 million lives.

👑 **1994** In South Africa's first multiracial elections the African National Congress wins a decisive victory, and Nelson Mandela is elected as the country's new president.

The Gulf War was fought to expel Iraqi forces from Kuwait. A U.S.-led multinational coalition quickly established air supremacy, attacking Iraqi ground troops who could find no shelter in the desert terrain. The war ended with Kuwait liberated, Iraq's leader Saddam Hussein still in power, and up to 100,000 Iraqi soldiers dead.

👑 **1994** Israel and the neighboring Arab Kingdom of Jordan sign a peace treaty, formally ending 46 years of hostility.

👑 **1991** Former Indian Prime Minister Rajiv Gandhi is assassinated by a Tamil extremist.

☀ **1992** Hindu militants destroy a 16th-century mosque on an ancient Hindu holy site at Ayodhya in India; more than 1,000 die in the ensuing Hindu–Muslim rioting.

✗ **1994** Russian troops invade the Central Asian republic of Chechnya, where Muslim separatists are campaigning for independence; heavy casualties result.

👑 **1990** Democracy campaigner Aung San Suu Kyi wins Myanmar's general election; the ruling military junta declares the result void and places her under house arrest.

👑 **1991** Mount Pinatubo on the Philippine island of Luzon erupts; 200 people are killed, and a wide area is devastated by lava and volcanic ash.

AMERICAS

EUROPE

AFRICA

WESTERN ASIA

SOUTH & CENTRAL ASIA

EAST ASIA & OCEANIA

1989–1994 A.D.

45

1995–2005 A.D.

AMERICAS

1995 The Southern Cone Common Market (Mercosur) comes into effect following an agreement made four years earlier to create a free-trade area among Argentina, Brazil, Paraguay, and Uruguay.

1995 A truck bomb planted by right-wing extremists destroys a federal building in Oklahoma City, killing 168 people.

1996 Bill Clinton is reelected, the first Democrat president to win a second term since 1936.

1999 A Senate trial acquits President Clinton of perjury and obstruction of justice.

EUROPE

1995 The Dayton Peace Accord brings the bloody civil war in Bosnia to an end; the state is divided between a Muslim–Croat federation and a Bosnian Serb republic.

1997 Conservative rule in Great Britain ends after 18 years when the Labour Party under its young leader Tony Blair wins a landslide general election victory.

1997 Researchers at the University of Edinburgh, Scotland, create the first cloned animal, a lamb named Dolly; she will live for only six years, affected by premature aging and disease.

1998 Voters in Northern Ireland and the Irish Republic endorse the Good Friday Agreement, bringing the prospect of peace after 30 years of paramilitary violence.

1998 Serbian paramilitaries ravage the Yugoslav province of Kosovo, conducting ethnic cleansing against the Albanian populace, but withdraw after NATO orders airstrikes against Serbia (–1999).

2000 Serbia's President Slobodan Milosevic is ousted in a popular uprising; he will later be indicted for war crimes and put on trial by an international court.

AFRICA

1995 Genocidal violence between Hutu and Tutsi tribesmen spreads from Rwanda to neighboring Burundi, where a huge refugee population has taken shelter.

1995 In Zaire, central Africa, an outbreak of the deadly Ebola virus, which has no cure, claims 244 lives.

1997 Zaire's tyrannical ruler Mobutu Sese Seko is overthrown by rebel forces under Laurent Kabila. The country is later renamed the Democratic Republic of Congo.

WESTERN ASIA

1995 Israeli Prime Minister Yitzhak Rabin is assassinated by an extreme nationalist opposed to his policy of dialogue with the Palestinians.

1995 The Palestine National Authority, led by Yasser Arafat, takes control of the West Bank and Gaza.

1997 Reformist Mohammed Khatami is elected president of Iran.

1999 King Hussein of Jordan dies and is succeeded by his son Abdullah.

SOUTH & CENTRAL ASIA

1996 The Taliban, hard-line Muslim fundamentalists, overrun the Afghan capital Kabul, taking control of Afghanistan after two years of fighting.

1997 Burmese democracy leader Aung San Suu Kyi is released from six years' house arrest by the ruling military junta.

Taliban fighters pose with their weapons in the Afghan mountains.

EAST ASIA & OCEANIA

1995 Despite international protests, France resumes nuclear weapons testing at Muroroa Atoll in French Polynesia.

1995 The Japanese port of Kobé suffers extensive damage in a major earthquake; 6,000 people die.

1995 Members of the Aum Shinri Kyo cult release nerve gas on the Tokyo subway, killing 12 and injuring 5,000 people.

British leaders formally return sovereignty over Hong Kong to China in 1997.

👑 **2000** Republican George W. Bush emerges the winner in a tight and disputed U.S. presidential election. He is reelected in 2004.

✕ **2001** On September 11 Islamic terrorists fly airliners into the World Trade Center in New York City and the Pentagon in Washington, D.C.; a fourth plane crashes in Pennsylvania. Around 2,750 people die in the attacks.

Serbia's attempts to hold Yugoslavia together under its own leadership suffered a crippling blow in 1995 when NATO launched air strikes on Serb positions. Late that year Serbia, Croatia, and Bosnia–Herzegovina accepted a U.S.-sponsored peace plan. Violence broke out again in 1998 in largely Muslim Kosovo.

✕ **2001** The United States leads an invasion of Afghanistan, whose government is accused of harboring terrorists.

✕ **2003** The United States launches an invasion of Iraq.

👑 **2004** Ten new countries join the European Union, bringing the total membership to 25.

☀ **2005** Pope John Paul II dies after 26 years as head of the Roman Catholic church.

AMERICAS

EUROPE

✕ **1998** The Islamist terror group al-Qaeda bombs U.S. embassies in Kenya and Tanzania, killing over 200 people.

👑 **1999** The African National Congress consolidates its power with an increased majority in South Africa's second universal-suffrage election.

✕ **2003** Unrest breaks out in the Darfur region of Sudan, where government troops and their allies kill some 180,000 people and displace two million (–2005).

AFRICA

👑 **1999** A major earthquake in northern Turkey claims 17,000 lives.

👑 **2000** Israel ends its occupation of southern Lebanon.

👑 **2004** Yasser Arafat dies and is replaced by Mahmoud Abbas, who renews negotiations with Israel.

👑 **2005** Iraqis vote in their first election since the downfall of the dictator Saddam Hussein, overthrown during the 2003 U.S. invasion. Kurdish leader Jalal Talabani becomes president of Iraq.

WESTERN ASIA

☀ **1997** Humanitarian worker and Nobel Peace Prize winner Mother Teresa of Calcutta dies in India, aged 87.

Mother Teresa visits a Calcutta orphanage.

👑 **1998** The government of Pakistan is overthrown in a military coup; General Pervez Musharraf becomes head of state.

👑 **2001** Pakistan is a major ally in the U.S. invasion of Afghanistan.

SOUTH & CENTRAL ASIA

👑 **1997** Hong Kong reverts to Chinese rule after 155 years of British sovereignty.

👑 **1999** East Timor votes for independence from Indonesia; after much violence it will achieve its goal in 2002.

👑 **2000** The first-ever meeting takes place between the leaders of North and South Korea.

👑 **2002** Islamic terrorists bomb nightclubs in Bali, Indonesia, killing around 200 people.

👑 **2005** An earthquake beneath the Indian Ocean triggers a tsunami that kills approximately 310,000 people in Indonesia, Thailand, Sri Lanka, India, and other countries ringing the ocean.

EAST ASIA & OCEANIA

1995–2005 A.D.

FACTS AT A GLANCE

African National Congress

Founded in 1912 as a civil rights organization for black South Africans, the African National Congress (ANC) grew more radical in response to continued government repression. In 1961 it launched a campaign of sabotage, prompting charges of terrorism; its leader, Nelson Mandela, was jailed for life the following year. In 1994, when South Africa held its first democratic elections, the ANC became the governing party.

Afrikaners

South Africans of Dutch origin, descended from Cape Colony's first white settlers, who still speak their own language, Afrikaans.

AIDS

The acronym by which Acquired Immune Deficiency Syndrome is commonly known. First diagnosed in 1981, AIDS rapidly acquired epidemic proportions and spread around the world.

Al Qaeda

Literally "the foundation," an Islamic terrorist organization set up in the 1980s initially to support *mujaheddin* fighters resisting Soviet forces in Afghanistan. In the 1990s Al Qaeda turned its attention to western targets, achieving maximum notoriety with attacks on New York and Washington in September 2001.

anarchism

Political doctrine proposing that humans can live in free association without the need for states, police, or armies. Some anarchists have embraced violence to further their goals.

Anti-Comintern Pact

Agreement concluded in 1936 between Nazi Germany and imperial Japan to oppose the spread of communism. Italy joined the pact in 1937.

apartheid

The Afrikaans word for "separateness" and the name of the system by which from 1948 the South African government enforced strict segregation of the white, black, and "colored" segments of the population. Its constraints included separate living areas, restrictions on travel, and a ban on mixed marriages.

Apollo program

U.S. space research program launched by NASA in 1961 after President John F. Kennedy challenged the agency to land humans on the moon by the end of the decade. Apollo 11's landing module, carrying two astronauts, touched down on the lunar surface on July 20, 1969.

Arab League

The League of Arab States, founded in 1945 to further cooperation and settle disputes among Arab nations.

Ashanti

The largest of the chiefdoms of Ghana in West Africa, annexed by Britain in 1901.

Atlantic Charter

Statement of principle drawn up by U.S. President Franklin D. Roosevelt and British Prime Minister Winston Churchill in 1941 stipulating the terms on which a peace settlement should be based after World War II (1939–1945). The charter renounced territorial ambitions in favor of freely elected governments and free trade, and vowed to disarm aggressors.

atomic bomb

Weapon constructed by scientists of many nations working in the United States under the leadership of J. Robert Oppenheimer for the Manhattan Project from 1942 on. Two types were developed concurrently, a uranium bomb and a plutonium bomb. Their use respectively against the Japanese cities of Hiroshima and Nagasaki in August 1945 brought World War II to an end.

Austro-Hungarian Empire

The central European realm ruled by emperors of the Hapsburg Dynasty after 1867, following the establishment of the Dual Monarchy—a constitutional arrangement whereby Hungary became a separate kingdom from Austria. The empire was dissolved following defeat in World War I in 1918.

Axis powers

Members of the Axis military alliance in World War II. Starting as the Rome-Berlin Axis, a political alliance formed between Germany and Italy in 1936, it became a military alliance from 1939 on. Japan joined in 1940. Hungary, Bulgaria, Romania, and the Nazi puppet states of Croatia and Slovakia were also members.

ayatollah

From the Arabic *ayat allah*, "token from God," the title given to an especially revered interpreter of the law in Iranian Shiite Islam.

Bahai faith

Proclaimed in 1863, the Bahai faith calls for the unification of all creeds. Followers believe that its founder Bahaullah ("Glory of God") was not just a prophet but a manifestation of God, along with Zoroaster, the Buddha, Christ, and Muhammad.

Balkan Wars

Two separate wars fought in rapid succession (1912, 1913) in the Balkan states of southeastern Europe. The first was primarily an independence struggle for peoples seeking to break away from the declining Ottoman Empire, the second a jostling for position among the liberated states. The wars ended in the final expulsion of the Ottoman Turks from the Balkan region.

Bay of Pigs

Bay in Cuba that was the scene of an unsuccessful invasion attempt mounted in 1961 by CIA-trained Cuban exiles seeking to overthrow the Marxist regime of Fidel Castro.

Blitz

The popular term for the German air raids on Britain in 1940–1941 during World War II.

Boer War

More correctly the Second Boer War, an earlier conflict having broken out in 1880. Fought from 1899 to 1902, it marked an attempt by the Boers of Transvaal and the Orange Free State to assert their independence from British rule. Britain finally prevailed, but a lasting legacy of hostility remained.

Bolsheviks

From the Russian word for "majority," the hardline faction of the Russian Social Democratic Labor Party, formed when Lenin split the party at its second congress in London, England, in 1903. The Bolsheviks took a leadership role in the Russian Revolution in 1917, subsequently changing their name to the Communist Party of the Soviet Union.

Boxer Rebellion

Uprising in 1900 against foreign intervention in China. Led by the Fists of Righteous Harmony secret society with the clandestine support of the dowager Empress Cixi, the rebels murdered foreign mechants and missionaries and Chinese Christians before being suppressed by an international force. The name came from the tai chi exercises practiced by the rebels.

British Commonwealth

Also known as the Commonwealth of Nations. Voluntary association of states that formerly belonged to the British Empire, established by the 1931 Statute of Westminster. Its independent members continue to recognize the British monarch as head of the Commonwealth.

British Empire
Empire ruled by Britain from the 17th to the 20th century, largely dissolved in the years after World War II. At its height the empire extended from Canada and Guyana to Australia and New Zealand, incorporating the entire Indian subcontinent and large areas of Africa.

Camp David Accord
The 1993 peace agreement signed by Israeli Prime Minister Yitzhak Rabin and PLO leader Yasser Arafat, brought together by U.S. President Bill Clinton at the presidential retreat of Camp David.

Chaco War
War fought between Bolivia and Paraguay from 1932 for control of the Gran Chaco lowland plain. Bolivia was forced to sue for peace in 1935, and Paraguay gained most of the disputed territory.

Charter 77
Czech dissidents who published a charter on January 1, 1977, protesting the loss of human rights in their country following the Soviet invasion in 1968. They included Vaclav Havel, president of the Czech Republic after the collapse of the Communist regime in 1989.

Chechnya
Troubled region in the northern Caucasus whose mainly Muslim people were originally conquered by Russia in the late 1850s. Fighting broke out in 1994 following a unilateral declaration of independence by Chechen separatists, whose aspirations to found an independent state have been fiercely opposed by the Russian government.

CIA
Acronym of the Central Intelligence Agency, the U.S. government bureau established in 1947 to undertake espionage and intelligence activities.

collectivization
In state-run economies the merging of small farms and factories to form large agricultural and industrial cooperatives under centralized control.

communism
Political ideology derived from the writings of Karl Marx (1818–1883) that has as its central tenets the communal ownership of property and the means of production and the creation of an equal society.

Conservative Party
In Britain the political party that traditionally upheld the interests of landowners and the church. It was known as the Tory Party until the 1830s, when it adopted the name Conservative.

Cuban Missile Crisis
An international crisis in October 1962 following the discovery that Soviet missiles had been placed on Cuba. After a week's standoff Soviet leader Khrushchev acceded to U.S. President John F. Kennedy's demands that the missiles be removed.

Cultural Revolution
In China a political movement instigated by Mao Zedong in 1966 to revive revolutionary zeal and overcome reactionary bureaucracy. The purges the movement unleashed, spearheaded by militant student "Red Guards," led to the dismissal and death of thousands of Communist Party officials. Mao was eventually forced to call in the People's Liberation Army to curb the Red Guards' activities.

Dalai Lama
Tibetan spiritual leader. The 14th (and current) Dalai Lama became a symbol of resistance to China's 1950 annexation of Tibet after he fled into exile in India in 1959.

D-Day
The day (June 6, 1944) in World War II on which Allied forces under U.S. General Dwight D. Eisenhower invaded German-occupied northern France to begin the liberation of Europe from Nazi rule. By the end of the day 130,000 troops had been landed on five beaches along a 50-mile (80-km) stretch of coast, at a cost of 10,000 casualties.

Democrat
In U.S. politics a supporter of the Democratic Party, one of the two main groupings that dominated the political scene through the19th and 20th centuries.

Druse
Member of a Muslim sect that broke from Shiite Islam in the 11th century. The Druse's close-knit communities remain a force in Lebanon, playing a significant role in the civil war of 1975 to 1991.

Dustbowl
Area of the south-central United States around Oklahoma struck by drought in the mid 1930s.

Easter Rising
An armed rebellion of Irish nationalists against British rule that took place in Dublin at Easter 1916. The rising was put down and several of its leaders executed, stirring sympathy for their cause.

East Timor
The eastern part of the island of Timor in Southeast Asia. A Portuguese colony from 1859, it gained independence in 1975 but was soon after annexed by Indonesia. A separatist campaign protesting the annexation finally achieved success in 2002, when East Timor's independence was restored.

ecowarrior
An activist prepared to take direct action to promote environmental causes.

enosis
A Greek word for "union," applied to the aspiration of much of the Greek population of the ethnically divided island of Cyprus for incorporation into Greece. Turkish Cypriots have resisted the move, causing decades of unrest and sparking a Turkish invasion in 1974.

Entente Cordiale
Meaning "friendly understanding" in French, an informal alliance establishing cooperative relations between France and Britain in 1904.

European Union (EU)
Known as the European Community (EC) until 1993, an organization of European nations brought into being by the Treaty of Rome in 1957 with the purpose of developing policies of economic and political integration. The original six members (France, West Germany, Italy, Belgium, the Netherlands, and Luxembourg) had risen to 15 by 1995. In 2004 the number increased to 25 with the addition of 10 new states, mostly former communist countries of Eastern Europe.

Falangists
Lebanese paramilitary group, named for a Spanish fascist party of the 1920s, that drew its support from the country's Maronite Christian community. The Falangists' hostility to the Palestinian presence in Lebanon made them natural allies of Israel.

Fascism
The ideology espoused by the nationalistic and authoritarian populist movements that emerged in Europe in the 1920s and 1930s. The original Fascist Party was founded in Italy by Mussolini in 1919, taking as its emblem the fasces, or bundle of rods, that was a symbol of power in ancient Rome.

Fifth Republic
The republic created in France by General Charles de Gaulle when he introduced a new constitution in 1958 increasing the powers of the president.

Fourth of May Movement
Nationalist campaign directed against foreign influence in China, sparked in 1919 by discontent with the award of former German concessions in China to Japan in the Treaty of Versailles. Students were at the forefront of the movement.

freedom riders
Racially mixed groups of demonstrators who toured the U.S. South in the early1960s to protest racial segregation, particularly on public transport.

glasnost
A Russian term, usually translated as "openness," used to describe policies introduced by Soviet leader Mikhail Gorbachev after 1985. They included greater freedom of information, more open debate, and détente with the West.

Great Depression
The economic downturn that affected much of the industrial world in the 1930s, triggered by collapsing financial markets and bank failures.

gulags
Labor camps in the Soviet Union in which millions died, especially in the years from 1930 to 1955.

Gulf War
War undertaken by an international coalition led by the United States to reverse the 1990 invasion of Kuwait by Iraqi forces commanded by Saddam Hussein. The coalition struck in early 1991, expelling the Iraqis but stopping short of bringing down Saddam's Baghdad regime.

Hausa
People of what are now northwestern Nigeria and southwest Niger. From the 14th century a collection of trading states, in the 1800s they were incorporated into the Sokoto Caliphate.

Herero
Pastoralist people of Namibia, dislodged from their lands by expanding German settlement at the end of the 19th century. Their 1904 uprising brought savage reprisals and their near extermination.

Holocaust
From the ancient Greek for a burned sacrifice, the term used to describe the wholesale murder of Jews, gypsies, and other minorities in countries occupied by the Nazis in World War II.

Home Rule
The demand that Ireland—united with Britain since the Act of Union (1801)—should have its own parliament to manage its internal affairs. The campaign was a major force in British politics from 1870 on. After 1918 the call for an independent Irish republic replaced that for home rule.

House Un-American Activities Committee
Committee of the U.S. House of Representatives that investigated alleged Communist subversion in the late 1940s and early 1950s.

Human Genome Project
Program established in 1990 by the U.S. Department of Energy and the National Institute of Health to identify all the genes in human DNA and to determine their sequences. The project was completed two years early, in 2003.

hydrogen bomb
A nuclear weapon developed in 1952 by U.S. scientists that delivered a far higher explosive yield (equivalent to millions of tons of TNT) than the earlier atomic bomb. The first such device was tested at Eniwetok Atoll in the South Pacific. The Soviet Union tested its first H-bomb in 1953.

Indochina
Former French colony in Southeast Asia covering the present states of Vietnam, Cambodia, and Laos. Growing French encroachment from 1858 on led to the formation of the Indochinese Union in 1887 from the protectorates of Tonkin, Annam, Laos, and Cambodia and the colony of Cochin China. French colonial involvement in the region ended with defeat and withdrawal in 1954.

intifada
The Arabic word for "uprising," applied to Palestinian attempts from 1987 on to drive Israeli forces from the territories occupied after the Six Days' War.

Iran–Iraq War
Eight-year conflict that grew out of a border dispute involving access to the strategic Shatt al-Arab waterway. The war got underway in 1980 when Saddam Hussein's Iraqi forces invaded an oil-rich region of southern Iran. They were finally repulsed after eight years of inconclusive struggle that left an estimated 1.5 million people dead.

Irish Free State
The name adopted by what is now the Republic of Ireland from 1921, when it was given "dominion status" (self-government) by the British, until 1937, when it became a sovereign state.

Iron Curtain
A term coined by Britain's premier Winston Churchill to describe the political divide separating the democracies of Western Europe from communist Eastern Europe in the Cold War period.

Japanese Red Army
Marxist terrorist group formed in 1970 that allied with Palestinian extremists, carrying out atrocities including the Lod Airport massacre of 1972.

kamikaze
Literally "divine wind," a word originally used to describe a typhoon that saved Japan from Mongol invasion in 1281. Japanese propagandists in World War II used it to promote a campaign of suicide missions involving pilots flying bomb-laden airplanes into warships of the U.S. Pacific fleet.

Khmer Rouge
Cambodian communist and nationalist movement led by the dictator Pol Pot. After seizing power in 1975, the Khmer Rouge launched a three-year campaign of terror that led to the death of two million citizens by execution in "killing fields" or in forced labor camps. Driven from power by Vietnamese invaders in 1978, it remained a potent guerrilla force until the mid 1990s.

Korean War
Conflict (1950–1953) arising from the partition of Korea between the communist North and capitalist South at the end of World War II. North Korea invaded the south in 1950 and made gains before being driven back by a UN force led by American troops. China intervened when UN troops reached the Yalu River, the border with China, and overran the South Korean capital at Seoul. After an outflanking landing at Inchon, UN forces regained ground; peace talks set the border between the two Koreas at the 38th Parallel, the postwar frontier, where it remains today.

Kosovo
An autonomous province of the former Yugoslavia in which the majority of the people are of Albanian descent. Serbian forces launched an offensive against separatists in the province in 1998 that was halted by NATO bombing in 1999, after which Kosovo was placed under UN administration.

Kurds
The once nomadic inhabitants of Kurdistan, a mountainous region now split between southeastern Turkey, Armenia, Syria, Iraq, and Iran. Since the late 19th century Kurds have campaigned for their country to be recognized as a nation-state.

Labour Party (Australia)
Australia's oldest political party, founded in New South Wales in 1891. It first won control of the federal government briefly in 1904 and formed several administrations throughout the 20th century. Famous leaders include Gough Whitlam, Bob Hawke, and Paul Keating.

Labour Party (Britain)
A British socialist political party that was formed to represent trade unions and workers in Parliament. Originally founded as the Independent Labour Party (ILP) in 1893, it became the Labour Representation Committee in 1900 and adopted its present name in 1906.

League of Nations
International association of independent states set up after World War I (1914–1918) to promote peace between nations. It was dissolved in 1946 and replaced by the United Nations.

Long March
A 5,000-mile (8,000-km) trek undertaken in 1934 by Chinese communists led by Mao Zedong to escape from their southern stronghold in Jiangxi Province, which was surrounded by Nationalist forces, to the northern region of Shaanxi.

Mahatma
Sanskrit for "great soul"; the title popularly applied to the Indian nationalist leader Mohandas Gandhi in recognition of his principled and effective campaign to end British rule in India.

mandate
In 20th-century history authority granted by the League of Nations or United Nations to one state to temporarily administer another nation or region.

Manhattan Project
Top-secret scientific program established in the United States in 1942 to develop the atomic bomb.

Marshall Plan
A program of U.S. economic aid designed to revive the shattered economies of Western Europe in the wake of World War II. Officially named the European Recovery Program, it was promoted by General George C. Marshall and ran from 1948 to 1952.

Mau Mau
A Kenyan independence movement mostly made up of young men from the country's majority Kikuyu people who launched an uprising in 1951, sparked by the arrest of campaigner Jomo Kenyatta. The Mau Mau revolt lasted eight years but was finally put down with great brutality.

Mensheviks
The moderate group within the pre-Revolutionary Russian Socialist Democratic Party opposed to the radical program espoused by the Bolsheviks. It had ceased to be an effective force by 1921.

Mercosur
Free-trade grouping set up in 1991 by Argentina, Brazil, Uruguay, and Paraguay, designed to remove customs tariffs, coordinate economic policy among member states, and establish a South American common market.

Mexican Revolution
Violent insurgency that broke out in 1910, forcing the resignation of Porfirio Díaz, dictator of Mexico since 1876, in the following year. The leaders of the uprising included the guerrilla fighters Emiliano Zapata and Pancho Villa. Diaz's fall was followed by three decades of political turmoil and civil war only brought to an end when Avila Camacho was elected president in 1940.

mujaheddin
Arabic for "holy warriors"; Afghan rebels who opposed the Soviet occupation of Afghanistan from 1979 to 1989. They atracted many foreign Islamic fighters to their ranks, including Osama bin Laden, the future leader of al Qaeda.

Muslim League
A political movement founded in 1906 to represent Muslim interests in British-controlled India. Under the leadership of Muhammad Ali Jinnah, it campaigned for separate Muslim nationhood from the 1930s. Jinnah became the first leader of Pakistan after partition in 1947.

NAFTA
Acronym of the North American Free Trade Agreement, signed in 1994 by the United States, Canada, and Mexico, and designed to progressively remove tariff barriers and restrictions on cross-border investment.

NASA
Acronym of the National Aeronautical and Space Administration, a civilian body established in 1958 to supervise U.S. space research.

National Party
Political party, founded in 1910 to represent the interests of the Afrikaner population of South Africa, that promoted an aggressive policy of racial discrimination and segregation. In 1948 it introduced the apartheid system.

Nation of Islam
Also known as the Black Muslim Movement. U.S. Black Power organization, established in 1930 by Wallace Fard Muhammad and revived in recent decades by Louis Farrakhan. One of its most prominent spokesmen was Malcolm X, who split from the movement in 1963.

NATO
Acronym for the North Atlantic Treaty Organization, an association of the United States, Canada, and several Western European states, formed in 1949 for the defense of Europe and North America from the threat of Soviet aggression.

Nazis
Supporters of the National Socialist Workers Party of Germany, led by Adolf Hitler (1889–1945), whose racist, and especially anti-Semitic, ideology was based on a belief in the ethnic purity of the German race. After taking power in 1933, Hitler built up a Nazi dictatorship that took control of the state at all levels; his aggressive foreign policies led to World War II.

nonaligned movement
A group of nations, mostly in the developing world, that pursued a policy of neutrality toward the superpowers (the United States and Soviet Union) during the Cold War.

Northern Expedition
A military campaign launched in 1926 by nationalist Kuomintang forces under the command of Chiang Kai-shek to overthrow the warlords then ruling northern China. Beijing was captured in 1928.

Organization of African Unity
Body founded in 1963 to promote cooperation between African nations. Its headquarters are in Addis Ababa, Ethiopia.

Ottoman Dynasty
Named for Uthman, a tribal leader who came to prominence in eastern Asia Minor in 1281, a line of rulers who built a great and enduring empire in western Asia and the eastern Mediterranean from the 14th century on. By the 19th century the Ottoman Empire was in decline, and it ceased to exist following defeat in World War I.

Pahlavi Dynasty
The ruling house of Iran from 1925, when Reza Shah Pahlavi was elected shah by the country's *majli,* or assembly; formerly a military officer, he had been effective ruler in Iran since 1921.

Palestinian Liberation Organization
Resistance organization founded in 1964 to coordinate opposition to the Israeli presence in Palestine. The PLO turned increasingly to terrorism following Arab military defeats by Israel in 1967 and 1973.

Pan-African Congress
Succession of conferences called from 1919 on to promote African unity and oppose colonialism.

Panama Canal
Canal across the Isthmus of Panama connecting the Atlantic and Pacific oceans; the canal opened in 1914.

Polisario Front
Guerrilla group formed to resist the occupation of the former Spanish territory of Western Sahara by Morocco and Mauritania following the Spanish withdrawal in 1976. Morocco has yet to relinquish its hold on the region.

Prague Spring
Short-lived reform movement that sought to liberalize the Communist regime in Czechoslovakia in the spring and summer of 1968. It ended in August when the Soviet Union sent in troops and tanks to crush resistance.

Prohibition
The outlawing of the sale and consumption of alcohol, as practiced in the United States from 1920 to 1933. The Prohibition era was inaugurated by the Volstead Act (1919), which brought into effect the Eighteenth Amendment to the U.S. Constitution, banning alcohol.

protectorate
A state taken under the protection of another state and thereby effectively under that state's control.

reparations
Compensation for war damage paid by a defeated state to the victor or victors.

Republican
In U.S. politics a supporter of the Republican Party, with the Democratic Party one of two groupings that have dominated the nation's affairs since the 19th century.

Rif Rebellion
A 1921 rising of the Rif tribes, inhabitants of Moroccan coastal colonies awarded to Spain and France under the 1912 Treaty of Fez. The revolt was finally put down in 1926.

Russo-Japanese War
War fought in 1904–1905 by Russia and Japan over competing claims to the northern Chinese region of Manchuria. The Japanese forces swiftly established supremacy by land and sea, annihilating the Russian Baltic fleet, which had sailed halfway around the world, at the Battle of Tsushima.

SALT
Strategic Arms Limitations Talks (or Treaty)—a series of negotiations between the United States and Soviet Union to reduce nuclear arms that took place from 1969 to 1979.

Sandinista
Supporter of the Sandinista National Liberation Front, a Nicaraguan guerrilla movement that opposed the dictatorship of Anastasio Somoza, winning power in 1979. The movement took its name from a revolutionary leader of the 1930s. The socialist government established after the Sandinista takeover became involved in the 1980s in a bitter civil war with U.S.-backed Contra rebels.

Saudi Dynasty
Ruling dynasty of Saudi Arabia tracing its origins back to the 15th century. From the mid-18th century Saudi rulers embraced Wahhabism, a strictly conservative interpretation of Islam.

shah
Persian for "king." Originally the title of the kings of Persia, it also came to be used by the rulers of other countries in South and Central Asia

show trials
A series of political trials held in the Soviet Union in the 1930s at the direction of Stalin, at which the accused made public confessions of their alleged crimes. The trials aimed to eliminate political enemies and terrorize the public into compliance.

Sikhs
Followers of the religion founded in the Punjab area of northwestern India by Guru Nanak (1469–1539). Sikhs believe in a single god who is the immortal creator of the universe and in the equality of all human beings.

Sino–Japanese War
War that followed the Japanese invasion of China in 1937 after the earlier annexation of Manchuria in 1931. Japanese forces overran most of northern China, ousting the Nationalist government from its capital, Nanking. Nationalists and Communist forces both fought the invaders, who finally left in 1945.

Six Days' War
War setting Israel against Egypt, Syria, and Jordan in 1967. Preemptive airstrikes gave the Israelis military superiority before the enemy forces could be deployed, bringing the fighting to an end in just six days.

Society of Muslim Brothers
Organization founded in Egypt in 1928 by Hasan al-Banna to counter what he saw as the growing secularization of society throughout the Islamic world under western colonial rule.

Sokoto Caliphate
Islamic state in West Africa established by Usman dan Fodio and his Fulani warriors following their conquest of the Hausa kingdoms in 1804. They went on to create an empire covering much of what is now north and central Nigeria.

Solidarity
Trade union that took on Poland's communist regime in a series of strikes in the shipyards of Gdansk and that later came to spearhead a mass campaign for political change. Banned in 1981, it reemerged eight years later as a force in the first multiparty elections held in Poland since 1947.

Space Race
The rivalry that developed between the United States and Soviet Union in the 1950s to be the first to develop a program for exploring space.

Spanish Civil War
Civil conflict that erupted in 1936 when a right-wing nationalist army led by General Franco attempted to oust the left-wing republican government of Spain. Franco's forces won, establishing the general as dictator of Spain until his death in 1975.

Spartacists
Members of the Spartacus League, a German communist group led by Rosa Luxemburg and Karl Liebknecht that organized an unsuccessful uprising in Berlin in 1919.

Strategic Defense Initiative
Often referred to by its intitals as SDI and popularly known as Star Wars, a defense initiative announced by President Ronald Reagan in the early 1980s designed to protect the United States by intercepting intercontinental ballistic missiles and destroying them in space before they reached their targets.

Sudetenland
An area in the northwest of what is now the Czech Republic that became part of Czechoslovakia after World War I. It contained a large German population and became a target of Hitler's expansionist policies. He succeeded in taking it over in 1938.

Suez Crisis
Crisis stemming from Egyptian President Nasser's 1956 decision to nationalize the Suez Canal, previously administered by Britain. In retaliation Britain launched an attack on Egypt with French and Israeli help, but was subsequently forced to call back its troops as a result of U.S. pressure. The canal remained in Egyptian hands, and British prestige was badly damaged.

suffragists
Also called suffragettes; women campaigning for the right to vote.

sweatshop
A poorly equipped workplace where employees work long hours for low pay.

Taliban
The Pashto word for "seeker," used to denote a militant Sunni islamic movement that originated in the seminaries (*madrasahs*) of northern Pakistan and gained control of Afghanistan in 1996, imposing strict Islamic law and suppressing all opposition. The Taliban regime was toppled by U.S.-led invasion forces in 2002 as a result of its support for the al Qaeda terrrorist organization.

Tamils
A people of southern India also established in northeastern Sri Lanka, where the Tamil Tiger guerrilla group has been fighting for a separate state (Tamil Eelam) from the Sinhalese majority since the 1980s.

Teapot Dome Scandal
Political scandal that rocked the administration of U.S. President Warren Harding from 1922, when Secretary of the Interior Albert B. Fall was accused of improperly leasing state-owned oil fields at Teapot Dome, Wyoming. Fall was eventually convicted of accepting bribes in 1929.

Tet Offensive
Surprise military offensive launched by the Vietcong and North Vietnamese Army against U.S.-backed South Vietnam in January 1968.

Transjordan
Portion of the Palestinian lands mandated to British control after World War I that lay to the east of the Jordan River. Transjordan gained independence in 1946, changing its name in 1950 to Jordan.

Treaty of Versailles
The collective name given to the series of treaties, signed in and around Paris in 1919, that brought a formal end to World War I. It broke up the empires of defeated Germany and Austria–Hungary and created a number of new countries in eastern Europe and the Balkans, including Czechoslovakia and Yugoslavia. The treaty imposed heavy reparations on Germany for war damage.

Triple Entente
An alliance signed in 1907 linking Britain, France, and Russia to balance the Triple Alliance of 1882 between Austria-Hungary, Germany, and Italy.

Troubles, The
A general term for the hostilities that divided the Catholic and Protestant communities of Northern Ireland from 1968.

Truman Doctrine
Principle expressed by U.S. President Harry S. Truman in 1947 that the U.S. would support "free peoples who are resisting subjugation by armed minorities or by outside pressures." The doctrine, which was aimed at countering communist subversion in eastern Europe and Turkey, gave formal expression to the start of the Cold War.

United Arab Republic
Political union that joined Egypt and Syria, although not geographically neighbors, in 1958 as a first step toward Egyptian President Gamal Abdel Nasser's "Pan-Arab" vision. The experiment proved short-lived, the Syrians breaking away in 1961.

United Nations
Organization of independent states that replaced the League of Nations after World War II as an international vehicle for the maintenance of peace and security. The charter establishing the United Nations was signed by 50 nations in 1945; the organization has since been joined by the vast majority of the world's states.

untouchables
The lowest order of the Hindu religious caste system, known as harijans ("children of God"). Regarded as impure, the untouchables were long discriminated against. Mahatma Gandhi began a campaign to raise their status, and the Indian Constitution of 1950 ended official discrimination.

Union of Soviet Socialist Republics
The USSR or Soviet Union, the former confederation of 15 communist republics occupying northern Asia and part of eastern Europe that was created from the Russian empire after the Russian Revolution of 1917. It was dissolved after the communist collapse in 1991.

Vietcong
A communist guerrilla organization active in South Vietnam from 1959 on that sought to reunite the country under North Vietnamese control. Together with the North Vietnamese Army, the Vietcong fought a long war of attrition against U.S. forces, emerging victorious with reunification in 1975.

Viet Minh
Vietnamese guerrilla movement founded in 1941 by Ho Chi Minh to oppose Japanese, and later French, rule in Indochina. Its effective insurgency led to victory at the decisive battle of Dien Bien Phu in 1954 and an ensuing French withdrawal.

Vietnam War
Conflict that ensued following U.S. intervention in a Vietnamese civil war pitting communist North Vietnam against the noncommunist south. Major U.S. involvment began in 1964 and ended with the withdrawal of troops in 1973. Two years later North Vietnamese forces finally triumphed, capturing the South Vietnamese capital, Saigon.

Wall Street Crash
Crisis that struck U.S. financial markets in September 1929, cutting 40 percent off the value of stocks in less than a month. The effects of the crash were felt around the world, triggering the Great Depression of the 1930s.

War of the Thousand Days
Three-year civil war in Colombia setting liberal forces against conservatives, who eventually triumphed in 1902.

Warsaw Pact
A military alliance set up in 1955 between the communist states of eastern Europe and the Soviet Union; also a term for the group of states that signed the treaty. The pact was dissolved in 1991.

World War I
Global conflict that broke out in Europe in 1914, setting the Central Powers—Germany, Austria-Hungary, and the Ottoman Empire—against France, Britain, and Russia (the Allied Powers). In 1915 Italy joined the Allies, while Bulgaria took up the cause of the Central bloc. The United States entered the war on the Allies' side in 1917. Fighting stopped with the Armistice of November 11, 1918, and peace terms were agreed in the Versailles Peace Settlement of 1919.

World War II
War between Germany, Italy, and Japan (the Axis powers) on one side, and Britain and the Commonwealth countries, France, the United States, the Soviet Union, and China (the Allied powers) on the other. The conflict was fought between 1939 and 1945 in two main arenas—Europe and North Africa, and the Pacific—with an estimated loss of 55 million lives.

Yom Kippur War
War that broke out in 1973 on the Jewish Day of Atonement (Yom Kippur), when Egypt and Syria launched a surprise attack on Israel. The Arab forces were repelled after three weeks of fighting, but Israeli casualties were far higher than they had been in the Six Days' War of 1967.

Young Turks
Group of intellectuals and army officers in Ottoman Turkey who agitated for political reforms, including civil rights for citizens and a national parliament. They forced through the revolution of 1908, imposing consitutional rule on the sultan.

Yugoslavia
A federation of Slav states in the Balkan region of southeast Europe, created at the end of World War I. It emerged from World War II under the communist rule of President Tito, but followed an independent line, refusing to join the Warsaw Pact. It broke up violently in 1990, when four of its constituent republics seceded. Serbia and Montenegro, the two remaining republics, declared a new federal republic of Yugoslavia in 1992.

Zionists
Supporters of the campaign to establish a homeland for the Jewish people in Palestine, launched by Hungarian journalist Theodor Herzl with his 1896 book *The Jewish State*.

FURTHER READING

Augarten, Stan. *Bit by Bit: An Illustrated History of Computers*. New York, NY: Ticknor & Fields, 1984.

Bix, Herbert P. *Hirohito and the Making of Modern Japan*. New York, NY: HarperCollins Publishers, 2000.

Brown, Judith M. *Gandhi, Prisoner of Hope*. New Haven, CT: Yale University Press, reprint edn., 1991.

Chafe, William H. *The Unfinished Journey: America since World War II*. New York, NY: Oxford University Press, 5th edn., 2003.

Chaikin, Andrew. *A Man on the Moon: The Voyages of the Apollo Astronauts*. Alexandria, VA: Time-Life Books, 1999.

Childs, David. *Britain since 1945: A Political History*. New York, NY: Routledge, 5th edn., 2001.

Conquest, Robert. *Stalin: Breaker of Nations*. New York, NY: Viking, 1991.

Conquest, Robert. *The Great Terror: A Reassessment*. New York, NY: Oxford University Press, 1990.

Cooper, Frederick. *Africa since 1940: The Past of the Present*. New York, NY: Cambridge University Press, 2002.

Dower, John W. *Embracing Defeat: Japan in the Wake of World War II*. New York, NY: W.W. Norton & Co., 1999.

Evans, Harold, et al. *They Made America: Two Centuries of Innovators from the Steam Engine to the Search Engine*. New York, NY: Little, Brown, 2004.

Figes, Orlando. *A People's Tragedy: The Russian Revolution 1891–1924*. New York, NY: Penguin Books, 1998.

Freedman, Lawrence, and Ephraim Karsh. *The Gulf Conflict 1990–91: Diplomacy and War in the New World Order*. Princeton, NJ: Princeton University Press, 1993.

Fromkin, David. *A Peace to End All Peace: The Fall of the Ottoman Empire and the Creation of the Modern Middle East*. New York, NY: H. Holt, 2001.

Garson, Robert, and Christopher J. Bailey. *The Uncertain Power: A Political History of the United States since 1929*. New York, NY: Manchester University Press, 1990.

Gilbert, Martin. *The Second World War: A Complete History*. New York, NY: H. Holt, 1991.

Gilbert, Matin. *Churchill: A Life*. New York, NY: H. Holt, 1991.

Gopal, Sarvepalli. *Jawaharlal Nehru*. New Delhi: Oxford University Press, abridged edn., 2004.

Kershaw, Ian. *Hitler*. New York, NY: Longman, 2001.

Lacouture, Jean. *De Gaulle*. New York, NY: W.W. Norton & Co., 2 vols., 1990/1992.

Laqueur, Walter, and Barry Rubin, eds. *The Israel–Arab Reader: A Documentary History of the Middle East Conflict*. New York, NY: Penguin Books, 6th edn., 2001.

Leuchtenburg, William E. *In the Shadow of FDR: From Harry Truman to George W. Bush*. Ithaca, NY: Cornell University Press, revised ed., 2001.

Mack Smith, Denis. *Mussolini*. New York, NY: Vintage Books, 1983.

Morris, Jan. *Farewell the Trumpets*. New York, NY: Harcourt Brace Jovanovich, 1980.

Service, Robert. *Lenin: A Biography*. Cambridge, MA: Harvard University Press, 2000.

Setright, L.J.K. *Drive On! A Social History of the Motor Car*. London, UK: Granta Books, 2003.

Shirer, William L. *The Rise and Fall of the Third Reich*. New York, NY: Simon & Schuster, reprint edn., 1990.

Short, Philip. *Mao: A Life*. New York, NY: H. Holt, reprint edn., 2000.

Sitkoff, Harvard. *The Struggle for Black Equality 1954–1992*. New York, NY: Hill & Wang, revised edn., 1993.

Smith, Thomas E., and Peter E. Skidmore. *Modern Latin America*. New York, NY: Oxford University Press, 6th edn., 2005.

Spence, Jonathan D. *The Search for Modern China*. New York, NY: W.W. Norton & Co., reprint edn., 2001.

Strachan, Hew. *The First World War*. New York, NY: Viking Books, 2004.

Tuchman, Barbara. *The Proud Tower*. New York, NY: Ballantine Books, new edn., 1996.

Tuchman, Barbara. *The Guns of August*. New York, NY: Ballantine Books, reprint edn., 1994.

Walker, Martin. *The Cold War: A History*. New York, NY: H. Holt, 1994.

Yahil, Leni. *The Holocaust: The Fate of European Jewry 1932–1945*. New York, NY: Oxford University Press, reprint edn., 1990.

Yapp, M.E. *The Near East since the First World War: A History to 1995*. New York, NY: Longman, 2nd edn., 1996.

SET INDEX